Welcome!

Welcome!

A Biblical and Practical Guide to Receiving New Members

Ervin R. Stutzman

Foreword by Marlene Kropf

HERALD PRESS
Scottdale, Pennsylvania
Waterloo, Ontario

Library of Congress Cataloging-in-Publication Data
Stutzman, Ervin R., 1953-
    Welcome! : a biblical and practical guide to receiving new
members / Ervin R. Stutzman.
            p. cm.
    Includes bibliographical references.
    ISBN 0-8361-3530-X (alk. paper)
    1. Church growth. 2. Non church-affiliated people.
    3. Converts. 4. Evangelistic work. I. Title.
BV652.25.S84 1990   90-38164
254'.5—dc20   CIP

The paper used in this publication is recycled and meets the minimum
requirements of American National Standard for Information
Sciences–Permanence of Paper for Printed Library Materials,
ANSI Z39.48-1984.

WELCOME!
Copyright © 1990 by Herald Press, Scottdale, Pa. 15683
 Published simultaneously in Canada by Herald Press,
 Waterloo, Ont. N2L 6H7. All rights reserved
Library of Congress Catalog Number: 90-38164
International Standard Book Number: 0-8361-3530-X
Printed in the United States of America
Book design and cover art by Merrill R. Miller

   3 4 5 6 7 8 9 10 96 95 94

To my wife, Bonnie, a wonderful companion and great encourager in the kingdom

Table of Contents

Foreword

When I was asked to join a neighborhood Bible study, I agreed without a moment's hesitation. The group would include non-Christians as well as Christians. I looked forward to meeting with my neighbors.

Little did I realize how much that Wednesday morning group would change my life. I had grown up in church and long been a practicing Christian. But I had never experienced the excitement of seeing new Christians take their first steps of faith. Nor had I walked beside new church members as they tentatively explored and then embraced a community of faith.

Week after week the freshness of reading the Bible with new Christians invigorated me. I watched the new members accept responsibility and begin to help shape our congregation's life. This stretched my own faith and expanded my commitment.

I discovered that welcoming new Christians benefits those already in the church as much as newcomers. This changed my way of looking at the church. The church is meant to grow. It is not meant to be a comfortable haven that remains the same year after year. New believers keep the church alive. So, if for no other reason than the congregation's own health, the ministry of welcoming new Christians deserves high priority in any church.

Ervin Stutzman has provided a sound, clearly written guide for churches of all sizes and stripes who want to welcome others. Using examples from a wide variety of locations, Stutzman helps us see what the church needs to do and be to make disciples.

He wisely pays attention to both inner and outer realities. For example, he does not neglect such nitty-gritty considerations as easy access to the building, attractive church signs, well-kept structures, adequate parking, and clean child-care areas.

But Stutzman also highlights the importance of vital spirituality, dynamic worship, and healthy relationships. No amount of fresh paint or well-lit signs will keep people coming to a church where Christ's presence is not known or the Spirit's power not experienced.

The book includes other helpful features: checklists (one list, for example, helps a congregation determine the warmth of its welcome), questions for discussion at the end of each chapter, and brief annotated bibliographies on each topic for anyone seeking additional help.

In a time when people often take church membership lightly and even dismiss its significance, Stutzman pulls no punches. He declares, "Belonging to a church is essential to discipleship and a vital spiritual life."

Baptism marks both a choice to follow Christ and a commitment to a fellowship of believers. This makes it imperative for churches to carefully prepare people for their life in the body of Christ.

In its early years, the Christian church understood the necessity of providing a nurturing environment for new believers. According to Hippolytus (A.D. 215), new Christians entered into a three-year apprenticeship. During that time, the Christian community hospitably received them, taught them the essentials of the Christian faith, and assigned a sponsor who walked with them on their journey and guided them into witness and service in the world.

If at the end of three years they were found worthy of membership, they entered a period of intense preparation for baptism. They then became members of the Christian community during an all-night ritual of celebration on Easter Eve.

The example of those first Christians calls us to give our best and most creative energies to the formation of new believers. *Welcome! A Biblical and Practical Guide to Receiving New Members* helps show the way. I hope many pastors, church leaders, and congregational participants will catch this book's vision for welcoming new people and expanding the church. The salvation of the church may depend on it.

> —*Marlene Kropf, associate secretary for congregational education, worship, and spirituality at Mennonite Board of Congregational Ministries*

Preface

This book grows out of my deep interest in, and concern for, new people who are coming to the church. I want them to feel Christ's welcome.

As a mission board administrator working with church planting, I saw how quickly new Christians could be welcomed into new churches. As an overseer for older congregations, I found it was hard for such churches to welcome new people. But older churches have much to offer new believers.

Many of the barriers older churches erect against newcomers are unconscious. We want to help new people feel welcome but don't know how. This book attempts to help both old and new congregations welcome new people into the communities which are Christ's body.

All anecdotes in the book are true stories. However, to maintain confidentiality, some names have been changed. Unless the context suggests otherwise, names used in anecdotes will generally not be actual ones. I've used examples from many different churches in widely differing circumstances to help illustrate the universality of the challenge to successfully integrate new people. Some anecdotes even travel overseas, particularly to the United Kingdom. They reflect time I spent in South Wales while writing this book.

I've heard many people who didn't find acceptance in the church tell stories of rejection. These stories have prodded me while writing. Rather than tell many such stories, however, I've shared numerous positive examples of individuals and churches who are welcoming new people. These stories can serve as models.

This book is more than a plea for different attitudes or programs in the church. Even such changes may not attract new people to our congregations. At the deepest level, church renewal is what the book is about. Renewal stirs us to share the good news regardless of cost. We'll open our door to people unlike us, giving them a place in the church and ourselves the task of helping them grow in Christ. My hope is thus not just to offer *information*, but to stir *transformation*.

I owe special thanks to Eastern Mennonite Board of Missions (Salunga, Pa.) for encouraging me to write this book, and giving me time to do so.

I also thank the many people who told me their stories or who have been resource speakers at various events. Worthy of special note are Al and Roberta Wollen, Bill and Chloris Lewis, Russell Chiswell, Philip Rees, Ian Burley, David Macfarlane, John Maxwell, Dale Shaw, Peter Wilkes, Ray Stedman, Patrick Baker, and Steve Morgan. Some stories are included; others influenced the book's direction.

Special thanks go to those who read and critiqued the manuscript. They include Keith Yoder, John Stoner, Samuel Thomas, Jonathan Booth, and Michael King, editor at Herald Press. Any shortcomings which persist are, of course, my responsibility.

Thanks, finally, to my wife, Bonnie, who bore the brunt of my time commitment to the task.

I hope God will grant special grace to all who read this book and enable them to find in Jesus Christ the answer to all life's challenges. May God help us all welcome many others into God's kingdom.

—*Ervin R. Stutzman*
January 20, 1990

Introduction

Thank you for picking up this book. It has grown out of a yearning to see new people warmly received into the church. Perhaps you want to minister more successfully to new people and need practical help. Perhaps you want to see the problem from a biblical point of view. *Welcome!* is an attempt to meet such desires.

The book may be used in small groups, as well as by pastors, congregational leaders, chairs of hospitality committees, and any other individuals interested in throwing congregational doors open to new people. Those studying in groups can hear one another's concerns, and together help make the congregation a more welcoming place. The questions at the end of the chapters can stimulate reflection.

Every church needs both "go-structures" and "come-structures." We're called to evangelize people on their turf. Chapter three deals with this. We're also called to welcome people onto our turf. That is the focus of the rest of the book. Many fine books have been written on evangelism, so this book deals primarily with the reception of people who have recently become Christians. It's equally applicable, however, to welcoming transfer members, since some "circulating of the saints" seems inevitable.

A friend of mine promotes Friend Day—a special day set aside to welcome new people to church. That experience gives members the opportunity to sit beside unchurched people during worship—perhaps for the first time. This can open their eyes to the perspective of others. They can begin to see how the church appears to the outsider. Similarly, this book is designed to open the eyes of church members who may never have been unchurched.

At times, as I try to open such eyes, I may seem to put older members in a bad light, particularly those who don't eagerly welcome new people. That isn't my intent. My goal is to help us all welcome new people with such love that they will stay—and become older members!

I'm trying to walk a fine line. I want to recognize that as we settle into our congregations it becomes harder for us to reach out to new people from within our own comfort. We then need to be challenged to reach out, to expand, to keep growing spiritually and numerically. We need to be reminded that churches that refuse growth are often choosing death.

I also know that, in a time of constant and often frightening change, people need some comfort and stability in their congregational experience. Pushing a congregation toward ceaseless growth and change may overload its coping capacities. And I recognize that some congregations, despite endless effort, never manage to attract the new people for whom they yearn. I don't want this book to produce yet more guilt and discouragement in congregations already guilty and discouraged.

However, while recognizing that some congregations need grace and mercy more than challenge, I've chosen (given my goals) to risk overemphasizing the need for challenge.

Congregations, like individuals, have unique personalities. We each have a certain approach to ministry. Newcomers used to different emphases may not feel at home in our church. Regardless of the kind of church we are, we will tend to exclude certain people.

Consequently, if our church isn't growing, we may find ourself excusing the lack of growth by appealing to theology. We may say we aren't growing because we're taking unpopular but correct doctrinal stands.

But a church needn't compromise its theology to welcome new people. It may simply be a matter of misplaced priorities. We may discover that the emphasis we have placed on certain doctrinal distinctives has blurred our vision for evangelism and has hindered our welcome of new people.

We may have a wonderful theology, but if it doesn't continually offer spiritual life to new people as well as to current members, this is a danger signal. It tells us to look for more creative ways of remaining faithful to our theology *and* ensuring it hasn't become a stumbling block that needlessly excludes.

A revealing glimpse of New Testament church life is found in Acts 5:1-14. The death of Ananias and Sapphira brought a pall of fear on the church, as well as the outsiders who heard of this terrifying judgment. The story closes with these seemingly contradictory words: "And all the believers used to meet together in Solomon's Colonnade. No one else dared join them, even though they were highly regarded by the people. Nevertheless, more and more men and women believed in the Lord and were added to their number."

People were afraid to join because of the fear of the Lord, yet they kept joining. This fellowship had managed simultaneously to stand for something *and* be irresistibly attractive to newcomers. Amazing! I pray God will grant each of us grace to join reverent awe with warm welcome to those yearning for an awe-inspiring God to worship.

Welcome!

CHAPTER ONE

Truthful Advertising

Jim Long,[1] a man in his late thirties, sat across a banquet table from me. A new Christian, he had just been released from prison. His conversation with the people who sat next to him intrigued me. He was a newcomer to their church; they were longtime members. He told them, "The church is going to have to change, that's all there is to it. If we're going to have new people coming into the church, we are going to have to change the way we deal with them.

"Just think of me. How are people feeling about me? And look at the people [mostly ex-offenders] I've been bringing to church. How do church people feel about them? If they don't want to accept these people, they'll need to take that 'Welcome' off the church sign."

As he spoke, his voice rose. His tablemates said they had never really noticed the church sign. But they agreed that if the sign said "Welcome," people should indeed be welcome. Otherwise, the sign should be changed or removed.

A few days later, I drove by the church building where these folks attended. The church sign announced in bold letters: *WELCOME TO ALL.* For most of the members of that church, the sign probably meant little. But for the new attender, the message was crucial.

After all, businesses are expected to honor the messages on their advertising signs and bulletin boards. Should we expect less of the church?

Like the man at the banquet table, many people in today's world long for a place where they can experience true acceptance and love. Sadly, people often don't find the answer through Christ and the church. Instead, they turn to alternative sources to try to fill the emptiness inside. Many turn to drinking and drugs. In his book *A Drink at Joel's Place*, Jess Moody asks,

> Can an average man *really* find more compassionate understanding at his church than he can at Joe's Bar? Is his pastor as willing to listen as a bartender?[2]

> A bar is always true to its name. When a customer comes in, they don't inform him that the only thing they serve is warm milk. If they were to do this, as many barflies would stay away from Joe's Bar as church members stay away from Sunday worship.
> The church had better come up with the choicest product brewed at Joel's Place, called "This is that."
> "This is that which was spoken of by the prophet Joel; . . . it shall come to pass in the last days . . . I will pour out my Spirit upon all flesh." Acts 2:16-17[3]

Al and Roberta Wollen, a retired pastor couple from Portland, Oregon, tell about a memorable visit to a church in London. They had flown from Portland and arrived in London on a Sunday afternoon to help prepare for evangelist Luis Palau's "Mission to London." When they asked about a place to eat, they were directed to the Ostrich Inn. As they prepared to enter the inn, they noticed a church building across the street. Since it was time for the evening service, they decided to attend—and eat afterward.

The service was already in session. A speaker and two others were on the platform. Four persons made up the congregation. Since the entrance brought the Wollens into the side and front of the sanctuary, they sat in the front row. The preacher seemed happy to see a 50 percent increase in his audience!

After the service, they found people were quite friendly and ready to converse. The church members proudly noted that the church had held Sunday morning and evening services for 400 years without interruption. In the course of conversation, the Wollens mentioned the circumstances that had brought them to London. They noted that they had stumbled on the church fellowship while on the way to the Ostrich Inn.

The fellowship turned cold. After informing Al and Roberta that the Ostrich Inn was a pub, the gathered group would no longer speak to them. These strict Christians treated them as outcasts because they had plans to eat at a public house. Yet no one offered to give them a meal or suggested another place to eat.

Somewhat daunted, the Wollens went across the street to discover a crowded eating house. When the proprietor heard their American accent, he announced their presence to the other customers. He warmly welcomed them to London and the Ostrich Inn. He went out of his way to make them feel at home. He showed them to a quiet room on the second floor, so they could relax after their long overseas flight.

As the Wollens left, they reflected on the stark contrast between the welcome they had received from the two groups of Londoners that night. Now they understood why the church had only seven people attending, while the Ostrich Inn was overflowing with people.

What should people rightfully expect when they visit your church? What do you offer to newcomers? Do you promise love? Acceptance? Forgiveness? Belonging? Identity? Fellowship? Security? Significance? Purpose?

If you're part of a local church fellowship, think about the "advertising" on your church sign, in your worship bulletin, in the newspaper, or elsewhere. Then think about the way you receive new people into the church. Might these people ever feel tempted to accuse your church of false advertising?

Dissatisfied Customers

Although the church is not a business, churches can sometimes learn from people in business. In the same way that businesses seek to maintain satisfied customers, churches seek to have satisfied members.

Most churches believe they are friendly and caring. For the most part, this perception is held by longtime members who enjoy being part of the fellowship. But what about the "dissatisfied customers" who aren't part of the church?

Years ago, a traveling salesman wrote a letter which appeared in the "Dear Abby" newspaper column. This salesman visited a different church every Sunday morning and night. He would sit near the front of the church, then wander back through the congregation at the close of the service, giving people a chance to welcome him. At the time he wrote the letter, he had visited 190 different churches. During that time, only three people (other than official greeters) had greeted him and welcomed him to their church.

What if this man had visited your church? What would he be saying to Dear Abby or someone else? Every "customer" who voices a "complaint" about your church may represent many others who have similar feelings but say nothing. These people may have chosen to "talk with their feet" by walking out and not coming back.

There are at least three kinds of "dissatisfied customers" who may have visited your church. First are the visitors who chose not to return after one or two visits. On what basis did they make their decisions?

Second are the people who attended your church for some time but are no longer active. What caused them to drop out?

Third are the people who transferred to another church, but who didn't change their place of residence. Why did they leave?

Consider the persons who are currently new to your church, who are still deciding whether or not they will stay. What kind of welcome are they experiencing?

If you're interested in determining how "truthful" the advertising on your church sign is, it may help to listen to some dissatisfied customers. Let's consider briefly examples of what one might hear.

Clara Sell tells the story of her visit to a new church. A woman approached her and asked her to give her name. She replied "Sell."

Since it was an unfamiliar name to her, the inquiring woman asked, "Zell?"

"Sell."

"Sell? Humph! What kind of name is that?" And the inquirer walked off, leaving behind her a shocked Mrs. Sell.

Kip and his wife moved into a new town and attended one of the churches there. After visiting for five Sundays in a row, they decided it wasn't the place for them. During that time, the only person who had spoken to them was the minister!

On Target

In the hustle and bustle of church life, it may take

all the energy members can muster just to keep the church program going. In the busyness, it's easy to lose sight of the real purpose of the church. The church exists not just for the sake of the members. It exists also for the sake of Christ, and for the sake of those who don't yet know Christ. The church is a place for new Christians to become part of the body of Christ.

Do New People Feel Welcome at Your Church?

The following questions can help you to determine the warmth of your welcome to new members.[4]

1. **Are there large numbers of people who have transferred out of your church and have joined churches nearby?**

    If so, this is a strong indication they weren't properly incorporated into your church.

2. **Is there a significant percentage of people in your church who have no specific role or task, or who don't belong to a small group?**

    If so, they're probably not vitally involved in the church. The exception to this rule may be older members who have been in the church for a long time.

3. **Is there a large gap between your church membership and the average worship attendance?**

    If church membership is larger than the average worship attendance, this indicates lack of involvement and lack of meaning in church membership.

    If average worship attendance far exceeds church membership, this is a healthier sign. However, it is also important to welcome these attenders into congregational membership.

4. **Is there a large gap between Sunday school enrollment and attendance?**

Lack of involvement in Sunday school generally indicates a need for better incorporation of new people into this small-group environment in the church. There may be need for better teaching, new classes, or a different curriculum.

5. **Is there a large percentage of the membership whose worship attendance is sporadic?**

   Sporadic worship attendance is one indication of a lack of incorporation. If church attendance becomes sporadic, there is a danger a person may drop out of church altogether.

6. **Do large numbers of your people feel left out?**

   Feeling left out is a sure sign of lack of adequate incorporation. Fully incorporated members feel a sense of belonging.

7. **Are there large numbers of visitors who don't come back a second time?**

   If you have a large number of visitors who don't return after their initial visit, this may indicate there is something in the worship service which puts people off. The obvious exception to this rule is the out-of-town guest.

8. **Is there a high percentage of new members or converts who have not been previously exposed to the ministry, programs, and people in your church?**

   If so, this may be an indication that your church is not being properly "promoted" by the members. Your community may not be adequately aware of the services your church has to offer.

9. **Are there a large number of new converts or new members in the church whose friends and relatives have not been exposed to the church?**

   The church grows primarily from contacts made by friends and relatives. It is thus essential that there be adequate follow-up to friends and relatives of new people in the church. This is the best pool of prospects for church growth.

10. **Are there people whose level of involvement has declined?**

    If persons are becoming less involved in congregational programs, they may be feeling left out. Lack of involvement in the church will soon lead to dropping out altogether.

11. **Are there unmet needs among the membership and participants in your church or community which are appropriate for the church to meet?**

    Persons will generally stay where their needs are properly addressed. Those with unmet needs may soon seek other places of involvement.

If you answered "no" to all the above questions, you may be doing quite well at welcoming new people. Nevertheless, keep reading. You will surely find some sparks of insight from the experiences of others who have worked to welcome new people. Or perhaps you should get a "second opinion" on the health of your church. You can do so by asking the above questions of a dissatisfied customer who knows your church.

Perhaps you were unable to answer many of the questions. To readily know the answers would require careful observation, and a deep interest and concern for new people. This book will help you learn to think biblically about the needs of newcomers. This can, in turn, prompt careful observation and planning in your church.

If you answered "yes" to any of the questions, keep reading. This is just the book for you!

For Review, Study, and Action

(1) Have you ever had an experience of not feeling

welcomed by a church? Briefly share with the group how it felt to be in that situation.

(2) Try to estimate your church's "welcome quotient" on a scale of 1 to 10, with 10 being the best rating possible.

(3) Talk to three people who have recently visited your church. Ask them how they were welcomed.

(4) Try to identify barriers which may keep you from providing a healthy welcome to new people.

(5) Respond to the story of the Wollens in London. Do you think your church is more or less welcoming than the local public house? Share any appropriate stories.

(6) If you haven't yet gone through the questionnaire above, do so now. Then go through it with someone who is new to your church. How do their answers differ from yours?

(7) Write down the names of 10 people who were once a part of your church but no longer attend. Are they "dissatisfied customers?" If so, try to place these names into the three categories discussed in this chapter.

(8) Ask at least two of the people on the list from number 7 above why they left the church. Perhaps you could ask them in this way: "I notice you no longer attend our church. Would you mind telling me why you decided to drop out?"

For Further Help

Assimilating New Members, by Lyle Schaller (Nashville: Abingdon Press). A practical guide to new-member assimilation by a seasoned church consultant.

The Inviting Church: A Study of New Member Assimilation, by Roy M. Oswald and Speed B. Leas (New York:

Alban Institute, 1987). This booklet is a helpful guide, particularly to mainline denominations.

Close the Back Door: Ways to Create a Caring Fellowship, by Alan F. Harre (St. Louis: Concordia Publishing House, 1984). A look at church dropouts, and how they can be reclaimed. The book also has practical advice on how to keep people from dropping out.

CHAPTER TWO

Good Samaritans

An Allegory

John and Sue Church enjoyed life with their two children, Matthew and Crystal. One evening, John read an article in the local newspaper. It explained the need for families to open up their homes to orphaned children. The Church family decided to invite two siblings, David and Sheila, to live with them. These two had been passed from one family to another in the hope that someone would give them a home.

The first few days together were quite enjoyable, apart from minor tensions. The Church family was elated. Life was more interesting with four children.

At the table one evening, Matthew said: "Wow, it's really neat to have David live with us. It's great to have a brother."

Crystal added, "Yeah, Sheila and I play with dolls together, just like our next-door neighbors."

John and Sue nodded approvingly. Helping these two unwanted children by giving them a home and family had been the right thing to do.

There were times of misunderstanding, of course. One day, John sent David to get a water hose from the pantry. David came back with a pair of Sue's panty hose! He had never heard of a pantry. John couldn't laugh about it. There were too many things David didn't know.

Well, it wasn't long before the Church family tired of David and Sheila. They were irresponsible at times, and slow to catch on to the "Church way" of doing things. And they started coming home late from school. They dropped by the Barrs', a family down the street, mixing with other children who came there every afternoon. Eventually the children didn't come back to the Church house at all.

John didn't worry about it. He assumed they were being taken care of elsewhere. David and Sheila seemed to fend well for themselves.

"After all," John and Sue reasoned with each other, "the new children weren't used to being part of a family before. So they probably won't miss it too much now."

John reassured Matthew and Crystal. "If David and Sheila want to be part of our family, they know the way back."

One day, the Church family received a visit from Stan Goddard, the children's social worker. Stan was shocked to learn that the Church family hadn't seen Sheila and David for more than two weeks. He was even more distressed to discover they didn't really miss the new children. John tried to explain to Stan that it was a lot of hassle to have a larger family. And that the new children just weren't making the necessary adjustments.

"Besides," he informed Stan, "the children are probably being taken care of. I imagine they're enjoying themselves just fine in that place up the street."

Stan was incredulous. He kept asking himself, "Is this really the family I knew earlier, who eagerly anticipated having someone new in the family?" It hardly seemed possible they had so readily rejected David and Sheila. But the Church family insisted that David and Sheila had chosen to leave. They hadn't been rejected.

After discussion, the Church family decided to release Sheila and David. They told Stan they would be content with their own family just the way it had been before David and Sheila came.

By now, you may have surmised that the story of John and Sue has parallels to the way some churches deal with newcomers. This story can serve as a reminder that the church needs to take responsibility for the reception and integration of new people into the fellowship.

The View from the Side of the Road

Jesus once told a story about a man mugged on his way from Jerusalem to Jericho (Luke 10:25-37). Beaten and stripped, the traveler lay on the side of the road, half dead. Two religious men came by and crossed the road to avoid the unfortunate man. A Samaritan, stepping outside of his people's usual animosity toward Jews, cared for him.

As modern readers of the story, we can imagine the scene. The beaten man lay on the side of the road, languishing in his own blood. We can guess what was going through his mind as he lay there, watching respectable people go by without giving an offer of assistance.

We can understand how he decided which of the three travelers was his neighbor. It had nothing to do with their race, color, occupation, theology, or personal holiness. Nor did it have anything to do with the warmth of their fellowship back home. What counted was kindness in time of need. By identifying with the suffering man's plight and meeting his needs, the Samaritan proved himself a neighbor.

Wishing to justify the way we welcome newcomers, we could ask, "Are these new people really my neighbors?" To answer that question, let's assume the point of view of the "one on the side of the road," the new person who is looking for a loving fellowship of believers. Who will be a neighbor to this wounded traveler? Will you?

We Are Stewards

A minister once told me he was relieved no new Christians had come into his church as a result of an area-wide evangelistic crusade. In his mind, it was better for persons not to come to church at all than to come and be rejected. He reasoned that the lay leadership of the church would have considered it too bothersome to adjust to new churchgoers.

How have you responded to God's entrusting of people to you? Should God entrust more new people to your church, based on the way you received the last six people God entrusted to you? If you're not really a welcoming church, are you willing to make the changes that will help you become that kind of church?

Affirmative Action

For some people, welcoming new people is a fifty-fifty proposition, a "meet me halfway" approach. This view is reflected in such comments as "I realize we have a responsibility as a church to welcome new members. But they must do their part!" Or "People who visit our church can see what we stand for. It's up to them whether or not they join us."

These sayings are akin to a young man proposing to a young woman: "I'd like to invite you to marry me— as long as you make all the changes to adapt to my lifestyle. I probably won't change much."

Happily married couples will probably agree that marriage works best when both partners fully commit themselves to make the relationship work. If either partner majors in tallying responsibility, something is wrong. True love seeks the best for the other, regardless of personal cost. In the same way, a loving church family will go out of its way to receive new people.

Sometimes new people come into a church with the expectation of being rejected, perhaps because of previous church experience. It takes a special measure of God's love and grace to welcome such people into fellowship. But after all, who is it that needs God's love most? Jesus said, "It is not the healthy who need a doctor, but the sick" (Mark 2:17).

On Foreign Soil?

Suppose you have just discovered your next-door neighbor is a devout Hindu. He is friendly, so you have gotten to know one another casually. Now he has invited you to worship with him at the Hindu temple. How will you respond? Will you go with him?

You might want to ask questions such as these:

"Will I be required to do or say anything, or can I just observe?"

"Will there be a foreign language used?"

"Will I be dressed differently from everyone else?"

"Will anyone else be there who is not a Hindu?"

"How long will the service last?"

Similar questions come to the minds of unchurched people when we invite them to a Christian church. Why not try to answer their questions ahead of time, allaying their fears and sparing them the embarrassment of having to ask?

When new persons first come to a church, they may feel they are invading foreign territory. The "strangers" feel at the mercy of the "natives." The "tourists" may present a passport and a visa, but the "customs official" has power to accept or reject their credentials. The natives may allow the tourists only a short stay or may deny entrance entirely.

The credentials required for belonging to a church may be related to family of origin, church background, color of skin, manner of dress, or similar factors. In all such matters, the new person is at the mercy of those already in the church. Members control most of the openness, friendliness, and welcome that new people receive. If these people reject the new person, for any reason, there is little or nothing a newcomer can do to fit in. That is why churches must not shift the responsibility for new-member incorporation to anyone other than themselves.

Being Advocates

A woman brought up in the church found it hard to understand why new Christians had such difficulty fitting into the church. Her pastor suggested an experiment. He sent her to participate in a bingo game. Since she had never been to a bingo game, the lady felt very much the outsider. She had to ask others what to do at every step.

The experiment worked. She didn't become a bingo player but did better understand the way new Christians often feel when first entering a congregation. She developed a desire to welcome such Christians.

To be quickly and fully received into the fellowship of a new church, new people generally need an advocate. An effective advocate knows both the new person and the receiving fellowship and works to link the two.

Several biblical examples illustrate the importance of advocacy. Saul came to Jerusalem, after leaving Damascus on threat of death. The church, "not believing that he really was a disciple" (Acts 9:26), didn't welcome him. They were suspicious and afraid of this zealous young man who had formerly determined to stamp out the church of Jesus Christ.

But Barnabas, the encourager, commended Saul to the apostles. Then Saul moved freely about the church in Jerusalem, until opposition outside the church forced him to leave.

Later Barnabas introduced Saul to the young church at Antioch, where they formed part of a leadership team. It was here that the first-known missionary team was formed (Acts 11:25-26). What a loss for the church had there been no advocate to introduce Saul to Jerusalem and Antioch!

The importance of advocacy is seen also in the biblical example of Onesimus's restoration to Philemon. Saul, now called Paul, served as an advocate for Onesimus, a slave estranged from his master. Apparently he had run away from Philemon, a house church leader who had been converted under Paul's ministry. Through the grace of God, Onesimus came to know Christ and became Paul's helper.

Later Paul sent Onesimus back to serve his former master, not as slave but as brother in Christ. The letter to Philemon is full of pathos. Paul employed every ounce of his diplomatic and persuasive power. He put his own reputation on the line. "So if you consider me a partner, welcome him as you would welcome me. If he has done anything wrong or owes you anything, charge it to me. I, Paul, am writing this with my own hand. I will pay it back . . ." (Philem. 17-19a).

We have no biblical record of Philemon's response, but tradition indicates that he received Onesimus back. Onesimus became a resourceful Christian and, finally, the apostle John's successor as bishop of "the seven churches of Asia." Imagine the loss if Paul had not been advocate for this slave with nothing to commend him, except the grace of God and God's people!

Jesus stands in history as the greatest Advocate. It is he who serves as Mediator between humanity and God and advocates humanity's cause (1 Tim. 2:5). Since Christ redeems people by his grace, how can we do less than serve as advocates, bringing new Christians into the full fellowship of the church?

Here are simple yet helpful ways ordinary people can serve as advocates for new people:

Sit next to a newcomer and explain the elements of the worship service.

Explain the significance of any announcements that are made in the service.

Introduce the newcomer to your friends.

Show the newcomer how to find his or her way around the church facility.

Let's Just Assume . . .

The material in this chapter may have challenged your assumptions about your responsibility to welcome new people. There are a number of assumptions commonly held by church members:[1]

(1) When a new member becomes inactive, the fault is generally the member's.
(2) About 60-70 percent of our new members can be expected to be active.
(3) An "active" member needs only to attend worship regularly.
(4) About 10 percent of the members should be expected to have a church role.

(5) The pastor is responsible for overseeing member assimilation.
(6) Numerical growth isn't a primary criterion for evaluating a church's success in ministry.
(7) The Sunday school doesn't play a significant role in new-member assimilation strategies.
(8) Newcomers will naturally feel the warmth and fellowship the older members share.
(9) Present classes and small groups can effectively assimilate new church members.

If all of the above assumptions were helpful and/or true, this book would be unnecessary! I encourage you to abandon all nine assumptions—not because they would render this book unnecessary, but because they can render a church cold and unwelcoming. Let me offer as substitutes the assumptions underlying this book:

(1) **Every church should be a receptive fellowship**. No church can be exclusive and at the same time claim to be under the lordship of Christ. A church can't pass off to other churches the responsibility for bringing new people to Christ and the church.

(2) **Most churches can improve their ability to receive new people**. Even churches which seem to be doing well say that they want to improve. I write believing that a deeper understanding of the need to receive new people will enable many churches to welcome new people more effectively.

(3) **Receiving new people isn't easy**. It takes time, energy, and money. Churches that have reached a plateau or are declining in numbers will find it a special challenge to really welcome new people. This book will point out many barriers new people face which may not be immediately evident to longtime members.

(4) **The responsibility for incorporating new people lies with the church, and largely with the leadership.** For reasons explained in this chapter, it's wrong to expect new people to be fully responsible for feeling welcome in the church.

(5) **The process of receiving new people will affect almost every aspect of church life.** An openness to new people should govern much of our church program, since evangelism is a crucial element in the church's mission. The following chapters will give many examples of ways churches have adapted their programs to win people to Christ and the church.

The Price of Growth

Many of us would love to see our churches grow. More committed attenders would help to pay the mortgage, staff the Sunday school program or nursery, or perhaps supply the missing tenor parts for the choir. A moment's reflection, of course, will reveal how selfish our motivation may be. This kind of motive won't take us far down the road of acceptance and love leading to real growth.

There is a definite price tag attached to church growth. It's a far higher price than most people realize, particularly if the church has a record of nongrowth. It's the price of *change*.

A middle-aged person humorously commented, "I guess we're all getting older, but what are the alternatives?" For people, there is only one alternative to old age—death. Churches, like people, can grow older and die, but there is an alternative. The church that continually welcomes new people won't die. But change and renewal are sometimes the required means, if not the end, of welcoming new people. *The price of growth is to change some of the ways we do things now.* Considering the alternative, is that price too high?

For Review, Study, and Action

(1) Review the story of the Church family. Try to find as many parallels as possible between the story and the situation your church faces in incorporating new believers.

(2) Try to view your church from the viewpoint of one "on the side of the road." What might a "wounded traveler" be seeing in your church?

(3) Discuss the idea of "affirmative action" for new people. In what ways can the church go out of the way to help new people feel at home?

(4) Have you ever been on foreign soil? If so, draw any parallels between that experience and the way a new person may feel in your church.

(5) Discuss the idea of advocacy. Think of the persons who have served as advocates for you, either in the church or in some other area of life. Whom might you serve as advocate?

(6) Review the first list of assumptions above. Do you agree or disagree that living them out can make a church cold and unwelcoming? How many are held by your church?

(7) How do you react to the assumptions in the second list?

(8) What changes may your church need to make to welcome new people more effectively? What changes are you personally willing to make?

For Further Help

Dropping Your Guard, by Charles R. Swindoll (Waco: Key-Word Books, 1983). The book discusses the individual and corporate attitudes needed to draw people close to each other.

Outgrowing the Ingrown Church, by C. John Miller, Ministry Resources Library (Grand Rapids: Zondervan Publishing House, 1986). This book can help church members to focus outside their own needs, to develop a ministry to others.

CHAPTER THREE

Reaching Out

Throughout his ministry, Jesus was occupied with one purpose: reaching people with the good news of salvation. He went to the people with his ministry of preaching, teaching, and healing. The Gospels give us glimpses of Jesus ministering in open fields, on the side of a mountain, in crowded marketplaces, even in a boat. He seemed as much at home in the public square as in religious centers such as the synagogue or temple. He seems not to have invited people to meetings or buildings. He instead invited them to follow him as a person. Even when people begged him to stay in one place, he moved on (Mark 1:38).

To accomplish his purpose, Jesus sometimes associated with people of questionable character. He even invited himself to their homes. For example, he told a tax collector named Zacchaeus he was coming to his house (Luke 19:1-6).

On another occasion, Jesus was having dinner at Matthew's house. Enjoying the meal with him were many tax collectors and sinners. Shocked by this unorthodox behavior, the Pharisees asked Jesus' disciples about their teacher's conduct. Overhearing the question, Jesus replied, "It is not the healthy who need a doctor, but the sick" (Matt. 9:12). Jesus made house calls!

But there is another important dimension here. In biblical times, a festive occasion at a prominent person's house was like a sideshow. Many uninvited guests peered in through windows and watched the action. It was inexpensive and sometimes exciting entertainment. So when Jesus mixed with tax collectors and sinners, he had a wide audience.[1]

Even today, the homes of other people are a good place to share the good news. Some of the people we can meet there might not readily come to a Christian's home.

Jesus not only modeled a life of ministry, he prepared his disciples to carry on his ministry of redemption and reconciliation. He said to them, "You are the salt of the earth," and again, "You are the light of the world" (Matt. 5:13-14). Both these word pictures portray *penetration*. Disciples of Christ who remain in their own little group are like salt in a saltcellar, or a candle with a bowl over it—unable to fulfill their true function.

The preoccupation of contemporary Christians with buildings and meetings isn't based on scriptural examples of reaching lost people. The concept of *going* to church isn't normative in the New Testament. Instead, the focus is on *being* the church in the midst of the world. Although buildings can be an asset to a fellowship of believers, they seldom assist in the task of penetrating the surrounding community with the gospel. Unchurched persons are best reached by the strategy taught, lived, and commanded by Jesus—penetrating their world.

But how can this be done? Let's consider several examples.

Will You Come to a Party at My House?

Evangelist Juan Carlos Ortiz often asks the question, "Why do we invite people to the one place we know they won't come?" He means the church meeting or building. He suggests that we invite people to our homes instead. This is a place to build relationships and introduce unchurched people to our friends from church.

Ortiz and others have been trying new ways to reach the unchurched—especially the well-to-do, whom the evangelical church of Latin America has not typically reached. A prominent member of the church will host a party and invite unchurched work associates and friends to attend.

One feature of the party is to meet Ortiz, international traveler and churchman. Ortiz then shares about his travels and presents a clear message of salvation through Jesus Christ. Using this approach, Ortiz has led many people to confess Christ as Lord and Savior and to join home fellowship groups.

From Pub to Place of Worship

Russell Chiswell, a minister in South Wales, has successfully led his church to meet the needs of industrial workers in his town. He insists, "You must build into your church program things that will build common ground with non-Christians." His church does this through special groups and events—usually held somewhere other than at the church facility. Since men and women in the South Wales valleys tend to socialize separately, the church plans separate events for women and men as well as combined activities.

The church began by offering a nursery, freeing women to go out. This met a real need. Now a "mothers and toddlers" group has emerged. It hosted a

onetime event called "hatches, matches, and dis-
patches," dealing with birth and parenting, challenges
of marriage, and facing death. The church has also offered special Bible studies and videos for women.

Events for men include a cricket team in the town
league. The annual banquet is "an absolutely brilliant"
event, according to Chiswell. It helps the church build
an image that men can be a part of the church. In their
solidly working-class culture, the church is sometimes
thought to be for women only. Many of their church
events are held in a local public house, where non-
Christians feel welcome and comfortable.

There are also many events to which both men and
women are invited. They conduct pub quizzes and
"poems and pints" on occasions. They have also
planned "60s and 70s" nights so that people could
reminisce about the "good ole days" and dress up in
costumes of years gone by. Barbecues are popular in
the summertime.

The object is to invite non-Christians to experience
the hospitality of church folks in a morally clean atmosphere, without being "too preachy." Chiswell cautions
that at these events the volume of the music must be
kept low enough that people can easily converse with
one another. Otherwise the purpose of the evening will
be lost.

It pleases Chiswell to see people waiting outside the
building on Sunday morning for their invited friends to
arrive. This suggests people are taking an active interest in bringing others to the church. The real process
of welcoming new people generally happens before
people ever visit a church service. If people simply
come into the church "cold," without having been part
of a Bible study group or special event, assimilating
takes much longer.

In 1983, Chiswell was the only person in his church interested in evangelism. There were only four regular attenders (out of 20) under fifty-five years of age. For the next year, he set aside two and one-half hours a day for prayer and intercession. Then for six months in a row, he preached on the theme, "You must be born again."

At first, Chiswell led others to Christ. These early converts came from within the church. Then they began to bring their friends to Chiswell, so he could lead them to salvation. Gradually, as they gained confidence, they led people to Christ themselves. But they brought them to Chiswell afterward, "just to make sure." Now, he hears about conversions through the grapevine. The church is at work!

Will You Join an Inquiry Group?

Joe Baker, a Baptist pastor in Fort Wayne, Indiana, initiated an interesting way of reaching the unchurched. He began by going from door to door in his neighborhood, seeking persons who didn't regularly attend church. When he found some, he invited them to an inquiry group—a series of four meetings to introduce people to his church. He also asked for the names of other unchurched people they might know and invited them as well. Then he asked a newcomer to host the group meeting.

In the inquiry group, the people first got to know one another and their past church experiences (if any). Baker then shared the gospel and explained the practices of his church. In the last of the four sessions, he handed out a church constitution and other church documents, including the yearly budget. There was no pressure to join the church.

In the first few inquiry groups, the group included

mostly unbelievers or nonchurch-attenders. Then the groups began to include a number of members from the church. The church has used this method for over 15 years. Beginning with only a pastoral couple, the church has grown to more than 500 people.

Why has this approach worked well? Perhaps for several reasons. First, Baker has an engaging personality and a real love for people.

Second, he enjoys leading people to Christ.

Third, the small-group setting gives an opportunity for church members to build friendships with people in their neighborhood who don't attend church.

Fourth, people can have their questions about the church answered in a nonthreatening environment. They can learn about the church without ever having to attend. Amazingly, more than half of those who come to the inquiry group end up coming to church!

Mothers and Others

In southeastern Pennsylvania, dozens of churches are providing a time out for mothers, especially those with young children. Meeting once weekly, these groups provide (in a nonthreatening environment) some of the best regular contacts between churched and unchurched women. Using such activities as Bible studies, crafts, and tips for practical living, these groups meet a vital need in the community.

Jim Petersen tells of the conversion of a Brazilian friend, Mario. They studied the Scriptures for four years. When Mario finally committed his life to Christ, he cited Jim's family life as a primary reason for making the decision. He remembered having a bowl of soup the first time he was at the Petersen home. The family had been somewhat unsettled, and Jim had corrected the children in Mario's presence. But in this incident, Mario saw Christ in a winsome way. He never forgot that incident, which pointed him to Jesus.[2]

Networking

Networking can be a form of upward mobility, enabling people to expand their contacts and business opportunities. But it's also one of the best ways to spread the good news of Christ and share your church welcome.

Arn and Arn, in a biblical and practical study, show how networks of relationship can enhance the potential of your church outreach.[3] They explain the concept of *oikos*, the Greek word for household. In the New Testament, there are references to people coming to Christ in households, which include relatives, friends, and work associates (see Mark 5:19 and Acts 10:24; 16:15, 33-34).

Working with existing relationships to find persons with whom to share the gospel offers several advantages. First, these networks of relationships proceed along natural lines. Since the relationships exist before the gospel is shared, the special gifts necessary for sharing effectively with total strangers or large crowds aren't required. Because the hearer already trusts the one sharing, there is often less resistance to the message.

It is important, of course, not to violate this trust. This means the friendship isn't formed with the hidden motive of eventually sharing the gospel. The friendship, instead, begins for its own sake. Then as it becomes appropriate for the friends to share their respective ultimate commitments, the Christian can share her or his commitment to Christ.

This leads to the second advantage. Witnesses can share with friends in an unhurried manner, waiting and praying for an opportune time. Again, when a person comes to Christ through the witness of a friend or relative, there is a natural means of spiritual support. Encouragement and sharing in Christ can continue where witness began.

A third advantage is the influence of relationships on the new Christian's choice of a local church. Statistics indicate that 75-90 percent of church members choose a church because a friend or relative attends there.

Fourth, emphasizing webs of relationship can result in the winning of entire families or households. Whenever a new Christian comes into the church, a new web of potential disciples comes into focus.

Expanding the Friendship Network

When new people come to your church, it's important to encourage them to invite their friends to attend as well. In this way, the number of prospects for your church will grow. If newcomers associate only with the people at your church, and drop their old friends, their potential to bring new people to church will soon diminish. Generally, after people have been a part of your church for three years, they are unlikely to invite new people to church except in special circumstances.

The church can arrange special circumstances, of course. Many churches have successfully used a program called Friend Day—a special day to bring a friend to church. Many congregations have doubled regular Sunday morning attendance on Friend Day. This is a helpful way to introduce many new people to the church.

Appointments Made in Heaven

Bob and Deb met at a bus stop in a large city. He was a young medical student; she was a teacher. Their eyes met briefly as they waited for the bus. He struck up a friendly conversation. They've been conversing ever since. In fact, they're happily married with two teenage children. Perhaps theirs is one of those "marriages made in heaven."

So far in this chapter, we have looked at ways to win friends and associates to Christ. But we're also called to witness to people quite different from ourselves—people with whom we wouldn't normally associate.

The New Testament offers examples of winning such strangers to Christ. Only God could have brought these people together. A textile entrepreneur and a jailer in Philippi, a treasurer from Ethiopia, and a military commander—all found Christ across cultural barriers (see Acts 16:6-34; 8:26-40; 10:1-48). All were matches "made in heaven." In each case, God arranged a special appointment which brought together two persons and resulted in an addition to the church.

Does God still set up "matches" today? While we have to acknowledge that God's ways are wrapped in mystery beyond our full understanding, it seems likely God is present in those many apparently chance encounters that lead to wonderful new relationships.

Getting Serious About the Unchurched

Pastor Al Wollen of Portland, Oregon, has seen hundreds of people come to Christ through his local church. He says:

> The degree of seriousness with which people pray for unbelievers is the seriousness with which we draw them into the church. The degree to which we get close to

God in anxiety for the lost determines how we pray for them. Christ came into the world to save sinners. You teach people how to pray for the unchurched by linking them to Christ and his concern for them. Pray the Lord of the harvest to send forth reapers into the harvest. You cannot say you are like Christ if you do not have a concern for the lost.

You can help to expand the prayer ministry of your church by identifying people who need Christ and putting their names on a prayer list. The congregation or a small group within the church can begin to pray for the people on the list.

Some churches have doubled their attendance by using this strategy along with the use of "prayer triplets." Prayer triplets are groups of three people who each pray regularly for three others who need Christ. In this way, nine people are prayed for specifically each day. In addition, each person prays daily for the other two members of the group. The triplet meets weekly to pray together and encourage one another.

A Place for Seekers

The Willow Creek Community Church emerged from a desire to win new people to Christ. Pastor Bill Hybels discovered that many church members were embarrassed to invite friends to a traditional service. They feared their worship practices were irrelevant and archaic.

Consequently, Hybels structured the new church around the special needs of the unchurched. Services during the week stir growth and discipleship in church members. But the Sunday morning service is designed to help *seekers* find the way of salvation. It aims to show (in language anyone can understand) how Jesus answers life's basic questions.

Congregational members invite their unchurched friends to these services. There is no altar call or other explicit request for commitment at that service. Rather, the members are taught to share the gospel with their friends, out of their own experience and interaction. The church also provides counselors when needed. Since Willow Creek was founded, this method has helped thousands come to Christ and join the church.

The idea of a *seeker's service* is new to many Christians. Not every church will feel comfortable using this method. But to appeal to the unchurched, congregations must provide someplace where seekers' spiritual questions can be addressed. If members of your church feel uncomfortable inviting unchurched friends to your service, perhaps you will want to change the present service or consider a seeker's service.

For Review, Study, and Action

(1) In what ways does your church penetrate the world of the unchurched?
(2) In what ways does your church facility help or hinder your outreach efforts?
(3) How often do you have unchurched guests in your home?
(4) What events does your church offer the unchurched?
(6) How is your church praying for the unchurched? In what ways might you expand this practice?
(7) What do you think of a seeker's service? How might your church implement the idea?

For Further Help

The Master's Plan for Making Disciples, by Win Arn and Charles Arn (Pasadena: Church Growth Press, 1982). This book explains the biblical background of the concept of households coming to Christ. It shows how modern Christians can use this principle to reach people for Christ and the church.

The Unchurched: Who They Are and Why They Stay Away, by J. Russell Hale (New York: Harper and Row, 1980). This volume grows out of research among unchurched people in America. The author shows that there are different categories of unchurched people, which must be reached by different means.

Witness: Empowering the Church, by A. Grace Wenger and Dave and Neta Jackson (Scottdale: Herald Press, 1989). This is a practical help to individuals and churches who desire to touch their community with a witness to Jesus Christ.

Won by One, by Ron Rand (Ventura: Regal Books, 1988). This is a book to help people minister to their closest friends and family. The author has helped equip hundreds of people for more effective personal witness.

CHAPTER FOUR

Making Disciples

Billy Graham is one of the world's most widely known and respected Christian leaders. Millions have heard him preach the gospel. Many thousands have responded to his call to commitment. Yet the churches have been able to assimilate only a fraction of the people who have made decisions for Christ at the meetings. In northern England, for example, a large number of young people made commitments to Christ during a major preaching mission in 1984. Now few, if any, attend a church. This is sad. Belonging to a church is essential to discipleship and a vital spiritual life. What went wrong?

For Christ *and* the Church

Christians must present the gospel in such a way that new people understand the role of the church *before* they make a commitment, rather than *afterward*. If the church is seen as an afterthought to the plan of salvation, people won't grasp the full importance of membership and participation in the body of Christ. Even a quick reading of the New Testament will demonstrate the centrality of the church in the plan of God. Consider two passages from Paul's letter to the church at Ephesus:

> God placed all things under his [Christ's] feet and appointed him to be head over everything for the church, which is his body, the fullness of him who fills everything in every way (Eph. 1:22-23).

> His intent was that now, through the church, the manifold wisdom of God should be made known to the rulers and authorities in the heavenly realms, according to his eternal purpose which he accomplished in Christ Jesus our Lord (Eph. 3:10-11).

God wills to bring everything under Christ's authority. Christ has chosen the church to be his agent. The local church exists to please Christ and extend his kingdom. The church has genuine power and authority under the rule of Christ. Each community of faith must submit to the lordship of Christ as revealed in the Scriptures, through the power of the Holy Spirit. When people accept Jesus as lord, and are born again, they need the nurture and care of a local church.

Too often the preaching of the gospel is separated from an emphasis on membership in the church. It's true that being a church member doesn't make one a Christian. But it's equally true that belonging to Christ means belonging to the church. Conversion and church membership are part of the same "package."

Russell Chiswell, pastor of a growing church in South Wales (noted in chapter three), declares he won't lead to Christ a person not willing to make an equal commitment to the church. Perhaps this is why 90 of the last 100 conversions in his church have "stuck."

Christ's Imperative

Jesus told his disciples:

All authority in heaven and on earth has been given to me. Therefore go and make disciples of all nations, baptizing them in the name of the Father and of the Son and of the Holy Spirit, and teaching them to obey everything I have commanded you. And surely I will be with you always, to the very end of the age (Matt. 28:18-20).

The imperative in this saying is to *make disciples.* The rest of this "great commission" relates to it. If converts simply make decisions to follow Christ, rather than becoming disciples, the work of evangelism is unfinished.

Baptism is closely related to discipleship. This event marks the beginning of new life, a pledge to Christ and the church. It's a public witness of dying to the old life and being born to the new (Rom. 6:1-4). It's the pledge of a good conscience toward God (1 Pet. 3:21). It may mark receiving the Holy Spirit (Acts 2:38) and joining the body of Christ (1 Cor. 12:13).

One becomes a member of the church by being baptized into the body of Christ. The act of baptism is both spiritual and social. It marks a relationship with God through Jesus Christ. It marks also joining a fellowship of believers. To be "born again" without joining a family of faith is like being born, then left on a hospital doorstep.

Teaching and obedience are also essential parts of Christ's plan for discipleship. The apostles were to teach their converts to obey everything Christ had taught them.

Bridgebuilders

People often come to faith in contexts outside the local church, including business luncheons, preaching rallies, youth concerts, church camps, and campus ministries. If those who respond to Christ have no local church, it's crucial to provide an advocate to introduce them to the church. Perhaps one could call such a person a "bridgebuilder."

Bob Reed served as a kind of bridgebuilder in a Brethren in Christ church in Canada. He was an enthusiastic elder in the church who loved to welcome new people. Most of the people knew him because he wore a badge with his name on it.

Whenever Bob's pastor led people to Christ, he encouraged them to call Bob with word of their new commitment. Even if it was late at night, Bob responded enthusiastically to such phone calls. The next Sunday, he met the new believer at the door and showed him or her special care and attention. The pastor testified that Bob provided an important helpful "receiving blanket" in his middle-sized church.

Whether or not bridgebuilders are appointed in your church, new Christians need some form of advocacy. How does your church welcome new people who have made commitments to Christ outside a local church?

Nurturing Disciples in the Local Church

The best way for evangelism to happen is for church members themselves to take responsibility to lead others to Christ. But how can this happen? How can the church develop an outreach which will draw people to both Christ and the church?

David Macfarlane, pastor of the Islington Evangel Centre in Toronto, offers an example. He looked for creative ways to win people to Christ and welcome them into the fellowship of his church. He has not been afraid to try new things. He discovered that non-Christians are most often present in the Sunday morning service, since this is the typical time people go to church. Consequently, Pastor Macfarlane always gives an evangelistic invitation in the middle of his Sunday morning sermon.

The first half of his message is geared to the unbeliever or the nominally committed. Here he tries to avoid "churchy" language and unfamiliar concepts. Then he gives an invitation. He invites adults who make a first-time commitment to raise their hands. They are immediately given some Christian literature and are invited to leave the service with counselors who meet with them in another room. Spouses of the respondents are invited to attend the counseling session. They often make their own commitment to Christ in that setting.

As the new believers are being counseled, Macfarlane finishes his sermon. He concentrates on the same theme but now focuses on those who are already committed. Using this approach, which balances a call to commitment with challenge to deepened commitment, the church sees an average of four or five adults make first-time commitments in each service.

"The key to successful nurture of new believers is relationships," says Macfarlane. "This is more important then taking a course or going through a study guide. After all, the church *is* relationships."

But how are these relationships formed? In this church, nurture groups are where new Christians find love and acceptance. There they also find special help to overcome problems such as alcohol or drug addiction.

Each Thursday night, the new believers from the preceding Sunday come to the church. They are personally interviewed to confirm their commitment to Christ and address special needs. At the end of this interview, they are introduced to the person who will lead a 16-week nurture group.

Whenever possible, the group consists of *two commit-ted Christians* and *three new converts*. This ratio and umber have proved key to the success of the nurture groups. During the nurture group sessions, people develop lasting relationships. In addition to the group interaction, new believers are encouraged by telephone calls and personal visits. At the end of the 16 weeks, "graduates" can join another 13-week course with a larger group. A broader range of relationships is established during that time.

Six months after committing their lives to Christ, these new believers have formed many new friendships. They have also been encouraged to invite their friends to church. Many of these friends become Christians and join the network of new believers in the nurture groups. Having friends come to Christ encourages new believers in their walk with Christ.

An Italian Catholic couple once visited the church after receiving a fruit basket from the church at Christmastime. They called to thank the church for the gift, and were invited to attend the services. They indicated that they had no car, so the church provided transportation. They came to church and made a commitment to Christ that Sunday, and joined a nurture group. Immediately, they began to invite others to come to the church. Within a matter of months, they saw 18 of their friends and neighbors make first-time commitments to Jesus Christ in the church services.

Of those who make a decision for Christ at Islington Evangel Centre, 75 percent choose to become part of a nurture group. Of those who join a nurture group, 95 percent stay in the church. As a result, the church has grown steadily over the past ten years.

One woman, a member of a neighboring church, often attends with a non-Christian friend. She knows there will be an evangelistic invitation in each service. If the friend comes to Jesus Christ, she invites her or him back to her church for nurture and fellowship. Neither church minds, since this helps build a spirit of cooperation. They believe there is so much evangelistic work to be done they can't afford to compete with each other. In the words of another pastor, "Arguing over who should evangelize in a neighborhood is like two ants arguing over who should get to eat the elephant."

Growing as New Disciples

We have noted the importance of building relationships between new and older Christians. It's equally important that new Christians develop a deepening relationship with Christ reflected in practical living. As a churchman once said, "No one can truly know Christ, unless he follow him in life." The apostles Peter and Paul both wrote to new Christians, expressing their concern for their ongoing growth.

> So then, just as you received Christ Jesus as Lord, continue to live in him, rooted and built up in him, strengthened in the faith as you were taught, and overflowing with thankfulness (Col. 2:6-7).

> Like newborn babies, crave pure spiritual milk, so that by it you may grow up in your salvation, now that you have tasted that the Lord is good (1 Peter 2:2-3).

Sometimes, new believers are disappointingly slow in their progress. The writer to the Hebrews seems to have experienced this.

> We have much to say about this, but it is hard to explain because you are slow to learn. In fact, though by this time you ought to be teachers, you need someone to

teach you the elementary truths of God's word all over again. You need milk, not solid food! Anyone who lives on milk, being still an infant, is not acquainted with the teaching about righteousness. But solid food is for the mature, who by constant use have trained themselves to distinguish good from evil (Heb. 5:11-14).

How can the church best help new Christians really become disciples? How can the church provide a context for steady Christian growth? Beyond the regular fellowship of a nurture group, how can a church lead a new disciple to become mature in Christ? These questions will help focus the remainder of this chapter.

Praying for New Believers

One essential ministry to new believers is to pray for them. In a sense, intercessory prayer is a form of advocacy. In his letters to new churches, the apostle Paul told the new Christians how he was praying for them. As you read the prayers that follow, think of a new Christian you know, and breathe the same prayer for him or her.

I keep asking that the God of our Lord Jesus Christ, the glorious Father, may give you the Spirit of wisdom and revelation, so that you may know him better. I pray also that the eyes of your heart may be enlightened in order that you may know the hope to which he has called you, the riches of his glorious inheritance in the saints, and his incomparably great power for us who believe (Eph. 1:17-19).

I pray that out of his glorious riches he may strengthen you with power through his Spirit in your inner being, so that Christ may live in your hearts through faith. And I pray that you . . . may have power, together with all the saints, to grasp how wide and long and high and deep is the love of Christ . . . (Eph. 3:16-18).

And this is my prayer: that your love may abound more and more in knowledge and depth of insight, so that you may be able to discern what is best and may be pure and blameless until the day of Christ . . . (Phil. 1:9-10).

. . . we constantly pray for you, that our God may count you worthy of his calling, and that by his power he may fulfill every good purpose of yours and every act prompted by your faith. We pray this so that the name of our Lord Jesus Christ may be glorified in you . . . (2 Thess. 1:11-12).

I pray that you may be active in sharing your faith, so that you will have a full understanding of every good thing we have in Christ (Philemon v. 6).

New Believers Class

Some congregations have had great success with a special class for new believers. On one hand, this may simply be another name for a nurture group. On the other hand, it may be more focused on curriculum materials to be mastered by the student. At the end of this chapter, you'll find a listing of materials you might consider using if you don't presently have such a class.

Al Wollen (noted in chapters one and eight) encourages churches to use printed curriculum materials sparingly for new believers. Otherwise they may feel they can't study Scripture without them. He believes it best to help them learn to study the Bible. He has training materials to help small-group leaders ask stimulating questions. These can then help new believers dig into the Scriptures for answers.

It can also be argued that written study guides give

students a chance to study alone and prepare a written lesson ahead of time. Students can then come together to share what they have learned. In this way, new believers can develop the discipline of personal Bible study. Whatever method you use, you must provide a structured opportunity for new Christians to learn and obey the Scriptures. And in every situation of life, teach them to ask, "What would Jesus do?"

For Review, Study, and Action

(1) Discuss the relationship between conversion and church membership. How can new Christians be taught the importance of the church?

(2) Think of the bridgebuilders, if any, in your church. How might they serve more effectively? For whom could you be a bridgebuilder?

(3) Consider the example of the Islington Evangel Centre. What appeals to you about the way new believers become part of that church? What would you ask the pastor if you had the opportunity?

(4) Do you give opportunity for people to make a first-time decision for Christ in your worship services? Make a list of opportunities your church provides for people to become disciples.

(5) How does your church provide for the nurture of new believers?

(6) Study the apostle Paul's prayers for new believers. Underline or make a list of the things he was praying for. In what way does your church encourage and practice prayer for new believers?

(7) What kind of new believers class, if any, do you offer? What is the ratio of new believers to older church members?

For Further Help

Being God's People, by Ervin Stutzman (Mennonite Publishing House, Scottdale, Pa. 15683-1999). This is a 13- lesson study for new believers.

Churches Alive, Box 3800, San Bernardino, Calif. 92413. This agency serves the local church with materials to help make disciples.

Improving Your Serve, by Charles R. Swindoll (Waco: Word Books, 1981). A helpful book on practical spirituality.

The Serendipity Bible for Study Groups, Lyman Coleman, editor-in-chief (Serendipity House, 1988). Using the entire text of the New International Version of the Bible, this study guide can help to stimulate group study on any biblical passage. It's as helpful for mature Christians as it is for those who have little acquaintance with Christianity.

CHAPTER FIVE

Sharing Space

A neighbor dropped by to visit Rosa, who was in the middle of a kitchen project. She invited the woman in, and they chatted in an adjacent room. After a few minutes, the phone rang, so Rosa excused herself. Then she forgot her visitor and went back to her project in the kitchen. Almost an hour later, the visitor casually strolled through the kitchen, saying, "Well, I guess I'll go home now." Needless to say, Rosa was embarrassed. Without intending to, she had crowded out her guest.

Jesus experienced something similar in the home of two of his friends, Mary and Martha.

> Mary sat at the Lord's feet listening to what he said. But Martha was distracted by all the preparations that had to be made. She came to him and asked, "Lord, don't you care that my sister has left me to do the work by myself? Tell her to help me!"
>
> "Martha, Martha," the Lord answered, "you are worried and upset about many things, but only one thing is needed. Mary has chosen what is better, and it will not be taken away from her." (Luke 10:39-42)

This story illustrates a simple lesson in hospitality. Mary acted as a true friend to Jesus, just by being with him. Martha was concerned about her guest too, as evidenced by her preoccupation with preparations for the meal. But her concern for the preparations nearly crowded Jesus from her attention.

The same thing can happen in the church. How many guests have visited your church, only to be left "sitting" by themselves while others are preoccupied with church duties? Newcomers who have been ignored may not announce that they are leaving. They simply slip out the back door and are never really missed.

Welcoming the Stranger

The first step in welcoming new people is to really "see" them, in the midst of all that surrounds us. As we focus on our own concerns, we miss seeing others.

Have you ever noticed the way your focus or perspective changes because of a certain experience? For example, after you have purchased a car, have you been more likely to notice other cars of the same make or model on the road? After my wife purchased a knitting machine, I noticed for the first time advertisements and magazines having to do with knitting.

A similar shift must take place in the lives of many church members for the church to grow. Their focus must shift to include people who are strangers or "outsiders" to the church. Let's suppose you were offered a $100.00 reward for every first-time visitor to your church you could identify. Would your focus change? Probably you would develop an entirely new awareness of visitors!

Throughout Scripture, God urges God's people to be kind to the stranger and the alien. Outsiders need special attention. Moses told the Israelites God cares for the stranger.

He defends the cause of the fatherless and the widow, and loves the alien, giving him food and clothing. And you are to love those who are aliens, for you yourselves were aliens in Egypt. Fear the Lord your God and serve him (Deut. 10:18-20).

To remind the Jewish people that God did not exclude people on the basis of national origin, the prophet wrote

> . . . foreigners who bind themselves to the Lord
>   to serve him,
>   to love the name of the Lord,
>   and to worship him . . .
>   these will I bring to my holy mountain
>   and give them joy in my house of prayer.
>   Their burnt offerings and sacrifices
>   will be accepted on my altar;
>   for my house will be called
>   a house of prayer for all nations.
>   —(Isaiah 56:6-7)

Later, in Jesus' time, there was a special area of the temple grounds dedicated as the place of worship for foreigners. Inside the temple walls, it was called the Court of the Gentiles. But it was in this place that the merchants and money changers set up shop, leaving no place for worship. No wonder Jesus made a whip and drove out the animals and the merchants. The area designated for prayer and worship for outsiders had become an open market for profiteering!

What is it that may be preventing you and your church from welcoming the strangers among you? How are they being crowded out of the place of worship and prayer? How might you be able to better include the stranger?

No Vacancy?

Have you ever looked for motel accommodations, only to discover there was no vacant room available? Some motels flash a "No Vacancy" sign to spare motorists the trouble of inquiry. But have you ever seen a "No Vacancy" sign in front of a church building, or on the door of a Sunday school class? Probably not!

Nevertheless, there are many ways in which a church may communicate "No Vacancy" to potential members, perhaps without saying a word. Even churches with some empty pews give signals to potential members, telling them there really is no space for them.

This chapter will explore ways your church may be putting up unconscious "No Vacancy" signs to newcomers.

Clogged Calendars

Many church people are busy. Their professional lives, together with church and civic activities, keep their calendars full of appointments and activities. People who enjoy telling others how busy they are and how much they are trying to accomplish may send the message that they have no time to build new friendships. This is a clear "No Vacancy" message to a person who is looking for a meaningful relationship.

When the people in your church are too busy with church activities, they will have little time to develop new friendships. Furthermore, since unchurched friends are the best prospects as newcomers to your church, the list of potential prospects may be quite small.

In a friend relationship, love is often spelled "T-I-M-E." The same probably applies to congregational newcomers. In their first few months of attendance, visitors may ask, "Can I develop friendships here? Where will I fit in? Am I needed here?" If they find satisfactory answers, they may stay.

As time goes by, they may ask a different set of questions. "Are my new friends as good as my old ones?" Does the group meet my needs? Is my contribution valued?" Again, if new people find satisfactory answers, they will probably stay. If not, they will leave or gradually become inactive. Seventy percent of those who become inactive do so in the first 12 months.

A researcher named Flavil Yeakley studied the church attendance patterns of new Christians among the Churches of Christ.[1] He found that the method of evangelism had much to do with the "keeping power" of the church. If the new believers perceived the one who shared the gospel as a friend, there was a much greater chance of them staying in the church.

Yeakley also discovered that new believers who stayed in the church after making a decision for Christ normally had at least seven friends in the church *before* making that decision. He found that, in general, people who made a decision for Christ but didn't stay in the church had few or no friends in the church before coming to Christ.

Our family has discovered that we must designate certain times on the calendar for developing relationships with new people. This helps us give time to something which is important to us but easy to overlook in the pressures of daily life. Putting it on the calendar emphasizes its importance in our lives.

Two Sides of Fellowship

When asked if his home group would be ready to receive new persons, Terry replied, "It has taken us six years to really get to know and trust one another. I wouldn't be ready to have a new person come." He felt that the group would almost have to start over if a new person joined. Long-term members of the group wouldn't be able to relate to each other with the same depth they were used to.

People who share their lives with one another over time may come to love one another deeply. They may enjoy sharing *in*side jokes and stories. It feels good to be *in*side a close-knit group.

But what about those who want to join the group, only to discover that group members would rather not welcome anyone new? These new persons will feel left *out*. Inclusion is one side of fellowship. Exclusion is the other. "Cliques" are so named by people who feel excluded from them.

When newcomers visit a close-knit group, they're likely to see the group's intimacy as a "No Vacancy" sign. Turning your back to a stranger or newcomer in order to talk to an old friend may also be a quiet form of rejection. We may wordlessly tell new people we have little interest in them.

If you want to know how friendly and accepting your church is, don't just ask a longtime member, who will view the fellowship from the *in*side. Ask a newcomer, who has seen the fellowship from the perspective of an *out*sider. Since outsiders are the ones we hope to draw into the church, it's important to understand fellowship from their perspective.

For eight years, Don and Judy McDonald taught a Sunday school class for adults.[2] The class steadily lost members until they decided to pray that God would send them new people. After a false start and some experimenting, they learned some helpful ideas, which helped the class grow about 10 percent per month. The class size tripled by the end of the first year. The following ideas, drawn from their experience, may be helpful to you as you make space for new people.

(1) Avoid inside jokes or humor. If someone tells a story meaningful only to certain participants, immediately explain it to the others so everyone can feel included.

(2) Always keep extra chairs or seats available for guests and latecomers.

(3) Avoid using natural selection when dividing into smaller groups. Instead, have group members number off, or use some other method, such as birthdays, parts of town, or alphabetical order of surnames. This will keep cliques from forming.

(4) If the group has been studying a series together, review briefly what has been done previously.

(5) Don't discuss plans or events which apply to only part of the group.

(6) Don't go around the circle, asking people to pray or read the Scripture aloud. Instead, allow people to volunteer if they desire, but make it clear persons have the choice to not read aloud.

(7) Discuss ways to meet the needs of newcomers.

Paul Y. Cho, pastor of the world's largest church in Seoul, Korea, doesn't allow the small groups in his church to be called "house fellowships." He believes that groups can too quickly center on themselves, with fellowship as the primary goal. In this fast-growing church, the primary goal is to reach new people and win them for Christ and the church. For this reason, small groups at Cho's church are called "home groups."

The home groups in Cho's church grow constantly by including new people and forming new groups. At the time of this writing, there are more than 10,000 home groups. In a combined effort, people in these groups win an average of 1,100 new people to Christ each month. That's a lot of people!

The Rule of 40

An urban pastor was disturbed because his church wasn't growing in numbers. He told me he believed people didn't really want the church to grow. They were happy with the congregation's present size. They enjoyed the sense of intimacy and fellowship with one another. If the church grew much larger, it would lose the sense of family togetherness.

In a small church, or in groups such as a Sunday school class, choir, or women's auxiliary, we feel most comfortable when we know everyone by name. Whenever a newcomer joins the group, unfamiliarity may make us uncomfortable. It takes effort to make room for the new person. Consequently, even though we may make friendly gestures toward the new person, we may spend most of our time with the people we know well.

New people intuitively feel this lack of welcome. They then drift away. This tends to keep groups fairly small, with 40 as a common limit. Some groups grow much larger, but 40 is an average size.

Using an analogy from biology, one might designate small groups as single cells. In relation to the church, a single cell may have these characteristics:

(1) Everybody knows everybody and the things happening in one another's lives.
(2) News travels fast to all members of the group.
(3) There is a sense of belonging.
(4) Everybody has a chance to contribute when the group is together.
(5) Newcomers are immediately noticed.

Heading for the Church Picnic

David Thomas, a retired minister, reared ten children. Some years ago, his whole family was on the way to a distant church, where he was to be guest speaker. As was their custom, the family traveled in two cars. They stopped for gas. Carefully assessing the situation, the attendant asked David, "Is this your family, or is this a picnic?" With a sparkle in his eye, he replied, "Yes, it's my family. No, it's no picnic!"

Had David been limited to one car, he could have taken only part of the family. But with two cars, he could take them all. In a way, the size and number of my friend's vehicles are like the size and number of cells or groups within a church. When the church has a picnic or tries to go anywhere together (spiritually or physically), people fall into groups. Single-celled churches want to get there in one group, with everyone in one large vehicle. If you miss the bus or if the seats are full, you'll be left out. New people can only get on board if there is plenty of room in the vehicle.

In contrast, multicelled churches encourage people to get to the "picnic" in many smaller vehicles. Everyone may be going in the same direction, but they get there in several groups. Any number of people are welcome, since they can hop into another vehicle and get to the picnic. The church picnic can keep growing and growing, because new groups are being added.

When they see all the groups, someone outside the church may ask, "Pardon me, is this a church family or is this a picnic?" You can reply, " Yes, this is a church family, and yes, sometimes it's like a picnic!"

Finding a Niche

It's a pleasure to walk along the seashore and explore the wildlife on the beaches. Birds and other creatures find their homes there. They live in cracks and crevices in the cliffs, hollow out a place in the sandy beach, or make a nest in the grassy edge at the beach. Each creature has its niche, a place to live and work.

Have you ever been chosen to fill a position for a team sport? In rugby or football, for example, there are a designated number of positions to be filled on the team. Each is a niche someone can occupy. Unless one is vacated, there is no room for anyone else to play.

Although the number of positions is not as rigid as in a team sport, one could say there are a limited number of niches available in any given group. The example of vehicles on the way to the picnic suggests that more niches could be created by forming new small groups. A niche is like a seat in a vehicle on the way to a picnic.

So new groups form new niches. Some congregations have difficulty starting new groups. People comfortable with their involvement in a small group or class won't readily abandon their niches. After all, they may have worked hard to find them. This is why it's extraordinarily difficult to form new groups in the church if one simply asks for volunteers from existing groups.

It's best to form new groups with new people coming into the church. There is plenty of space available in a new group, and no one has to give up a niche to join the group. Another advantage is that everyone has an equal chance of being on the *in*side of a fellowship which is just beginning.

People regularly leave the church, either because they are moving, are transferring to another church, or are becoming inactive. And, of course, some people die. Just to maintain the membership of a church at the same level requires a constant stream of new people.

But unless these new people find niches within your church, they'll find their way out the back door.

In my boyhood hometown, the visitors' bureau has recently adopted a new slogan—*Come Share Our Space!* These words are painted on the water tower and posted on the Convention Center. Brochures and advertisements use the same inviting words. Cities and towns, like churches, cannot survive without new people. If you want your church to grow, you must communicate loudly and clearly to newcomers—*Come Share Our Space!*

For Review, Study, and Action

(1) How busy are the people in your church? Check your calendar to see how much time you have invested in recent newcomers to your church. How much space is there in your life for new people?

(2) Have you ever looked at a clique and wished you were an insider? Describe your feelings as you watched the close fellowship of some intimate group. How might a newcomer to your church feel about the fellowship opportunities in your church?

(3) Discuss the idea of the two sides of fellowship. Try to make a list of ways in which insiders and outsiders in a group may see things differently.

(4) Review the story of David and his family. Which way does your church go to the church picnic?

(5) How many niches are there in your church? How might you increase the number of niches?

(6) Ask two or three recent visitors to your church how they perceived the fellowship in your church. How did they perceive the possibility of finding niches?

(7) Make a list of the people whom you might invite to your church. Invite two people at church to join you in prayer for the people on your list.

(8) Discuss the kind of special events your church might be able to host that would attract new people.

For Further Help

Friend Day, published by Church Growth Institute, Lynchburg, Va. The packet contains four cassette tapes and instructions, along with samples and reproducible sheets to guide a congregation in planning a special day to invite friends.

People Spots, by James W. Moss, Sr. (Eastern Pa. Conference Churches of God, 1988). Chapter three explains the dynamics of small groups within the church.

Three Times Three Equals Twelve, by Brian Mills (Eastbourne, England: Kingsway Publications, 1986). The originator of the concept of prayer triplets explains their use. The book is an inspirational and practical guide to prayer for individuals and communities of faith.

Tyranny of the Urgent, by Charles Hummel (Downers Grove: InterVarsity Press, 1967). This little booklet is about priorities and the use of time. The author uses the example of Jesus Christ to urge his readers to plan for the important things in life, not just the urgent ones.

CHAPTER SIX

Easy Access

Gordon and Joan were invited to a 25th wedding anniversary celebration. They were given general directions to the church where the celebration was to be held. "It's an old, established church. Anyone in the neighborhood can direct you there," they were told. But they couldn't find the church, despite numerous inquiries, and returned home disappointed.

Church people often assume everyone in the neighborhood knows where the church is located. One church consultant enjoyed exposing this mistaken assumption. When he was invited to a church, he would play a little game. Standing on the sidewalk not far from the church, he would ask passersby, "Can you help me find Oak Lane Baptist Church [or whatever]?" Many couldn't help. Later, as he met with the church, he would tell of his experience.

Obviously, if people don't know how to get to your place of worship, they won't come. And if new people experience difficulty finding their way around in your facilities, they may not return. How do you help newcomers get to and around your facilities? In what ways do your facilities enhance the welcome you give? Focus on these questions as you read this chapter.

Helping People Find Your Place of Worship

An evangelical church once mailed an advertising brochure to our home. The attractively designed brochure told about the church program. One essential bit of information was missing, however. There was no address or phone number. As a newcomer to the community, I had no idea where the church was located. I looked carefully for a listing in the phone directory, without success.

Perhaps it was a simple oversight, or a printer's error. Nevertheless, it's common for churches to advertise without addresses or phone numbers. They assume everyone knows where they are. Such advertisements announce loudly and clearly, "You're welcome if you know where we are. If not, find out yourself!"

The best way to help people find your meeting place is to bring them or accompany them. When you must give verbal or written directions, make them clear. "You can't miss it" usually means you most certainly will. Some church brochures include clearly drawn maps. These can be helpful, particularly if your church facilities aren't on a main street. A clearly drawn map says, "We want you to find us! You *are* welcome!"

Church Signs

A sign tells a lot about an establishment, be it a place of business or a church. The sign is the primary information many people have until they enter the building. Many churches have drab-looking signs, or none at all. And many church signs aren't lit at night, making buildings hard to find on winter evenings.

Good signs say you expect new people, who need such information, to attend. Good signs say *Welcome!*

Which Door?

Have you ever been confused by doors in unfamiliar church surroundings? On a Sunday morning visit to a neighboring church, I found a middle-aged couple standing outside. It was the time between the education hour and the morning worship service.

I introduced myself and asked if I could help. They said they were waiting for someone to show them which door they should use to enter the building. Regular members of this church would probably find this humorous or puzzling. But to these first-time guests, it was an important question: "Which door shall we use?"

The Open Door Christian Church meets in a gymnasium. Ironically, they lock the regular entrance door during the worship service! The only way late worshipers can enter is to walk around the building and find another place to come in. To thwart petty theft of coats and other belongings, this church has closed the door to people who don't know when or where to come in. The Open Door is shut to many!

Are all the entrances to your place of worship clearly marked? Are all the doors inside the building marked? Can guests find their way to the bathroom without embarrassment? Clearly marked doors help new people feel welcome. They help people find their way into your church facility *and* into your fellowship.

The Building

What first impressions does your building create? Does it look cared for or run-down? The exterior and interior condition often says something about the self-esteem or morale of a congregation. It's particularly easy to overlook peeling paint or unfinished decorating work when one worships in the building every Sunday.

Indeed, people who love each other deeply will meet under almost any conditions and in any facility.

But new people notice the more visible things. Is the grass cut? Is the front gate in good repair? Are the windows clean? These small things can make the difference between an inviting church and one that will make a guest feel like something is wrong.

A Place to Sit

Our family of five once attended a church in a capital city. The auditorium was designed in theater style, with up to 27 seats in long rows of flip-up chairs. There was no middle aisle. The seats were close to each other front to back. It was difficult for people to move past others already seated, even if persons stood up. There was little space for standing or moving.

Consequently, the middle section of the building was sparsely filled. Persons chose to sit near the two ends of the rows, because it took much less effort. The physical arrangement of the building greatly hampered fellowship and movement. In case of fire, it would have been hard to evacuate the building safely.

A room's seating arrangements make a difference in normal seating capacity. Most people don't like to sit too close together. This is perhaps one reason why the seats in a church building are often sparsely filled. Most churches don't grow in average attendance beyond 80 percent of the seating capacity in the sanctuary.

In a study of 700 churches in America, James Moss discovered that the *average* attendance over a year's time was 57 percent of capacity. He concluded that people generally prefer at least 25 inches of pew space. He asserts that newcomers won't feel comfortable unless there is that much pew space available.[1]

One can easily tell something about the body life of a church by observing the seating patterns. If people leave the front seats empty and scatter to fringes, it often indicates that people don't relate closely to each other. In contrast, when people come early to get a front seat, and the seats are full, this suggests expectancy in worship and eagerness to be with others. Newcomers can sense the difference from the moment they enter the place of worship. What does the seating pattern in your church communicate to a newcomer?

Parking

In today's world, most people drive to church. As pollution and congestion mount, we may learn to end our love affair with cars. But for now, parking is a problem for many fellowships. Where church buildings were constructed before the common use of cars, there may be no provision for off-street parking. As businesses build new stores on the outskirts of town, people become used to ample parking space. In many churches, the undersized parking lot is full, but the building could hold many more people. How a church provides for hospitality in the parking lot has become a major factor in church growth, particularly for large churches.

John Maxwell, pastor of a growing church in California, emphasizes the importance of servanthood and self-sacrifice in regard to parking spaces. As pastor, he could demand a choice, reserved spot for his car. Instead, he parks more than a block away and walks to church to leave space for guests. Willingness to leave the better parking spaces for others has now become one evidence of Christian commitment for the leaders and members in his church.

Similarly, South Hills Community Church uses a satellite parking lot. Members ride a shuttle bus in order to leave parking spaces for guests. This is part of the church's definition of hospitality.

Health buffs know the value of walking. To park at a distance from the church may prove to be healthier—both physically and spiritually—than to "hog the best space." Furthermore, it communicates clearly to new people, "Welcome! Share our space!"

Some congregations provide ushers outside the building to assist the aged or physically impaired, particularly in bad weather. Stepping up to an automobile to help a person across an icy pavement is a great way to say *Welcome!*

Ushers in the parking lot can help extend your church welcome in other ways. Dale Shaw tells the story of Willis, an unchurched man who had been invited by a friend to visit his church.

One Sunday morning, Willis and his wife drove to the church. As they pulled into the parking lot, Willis lost his courage and decided he couldn't cope with the church service. He drove around the building, intending to leave by a second driveway. But a parking usher stepped up to the car with a friendly smile. Extending a warm welcome through the open window, the usher directed the visitor to a parking space. With fresh courage, Willis parked and came to the service.

Not long after, Willis confessed Christ as Savior and Lord and joined the church. He is now an elder. The usher in the parking lot removed a barrier which would otherwise have blocked the way for this man to find Christ and the church.

The Worship Center, a large growing church in Pennsylvania, is located on a busy street. Each Sunday, traffic guides help drivers to get out of the parking lot and safely on their way. They want to leave a good "last impression" of the worship service.

The Nursery

If you drive to the new United Methodist church near Lancaster, Pennsylvania, you might notice the nursery first. The large room faces the street through a huge plate-glass window. The pastor has a heart for mothers, who often stay away from the church because it's more of a hassle to go than to stay at home. Good nursery facilities communicate *Welcome!* to tired mothers and energetic children. Even shopping centers and banks know that you reach parents' hearts by caring for their children.

A good nursery can tip the balance in favor of your church if a young family is trying to decide where to attend. Here are factors to consider when providing for the needs of parents and children:

(1) Think of the nursery as a ministry. That's what it's meant to be.
(2) Provide a quiet place where babies can sleep undisturbed.
(3) Provide a place where young children can play safely.
(4) Provide for easy parental access between the nursery and the worship service.
(5) Provide running water if possible.
(6) Provide a place to change diapers.
(7) Provide quality toys and furnishings. Old, worn-out, or broken things communicate that the nursery is second-class.
(8) Make sure the facilities are clean. Some parents will make their decision on this basis alone.

Special Facilities

How does your church reach out to people with physical impairments? Such folks often face extraordinary barriers to access in the church. In addition to the negative attitudes of some church members, they may face actual physical barriers, such as stairways. Aged people may need special assistance to park a car or to negotiate steps.

Persons confined to a wheelchair may find it difficult to make their way around the building because of narrow aisles or doorways, series of steps, or lack of adequate toilet facilities. A wheelchair ramp outside a church facility says *Welcome!* to people who can't walk on their own.

Mike King suffered a tragic accident as a young teenager. Vital nerves in his neck were severed, and he lost the use of his lower limbs. But this strong young man didn't let misfortune overwhelm him. To highlight the special needs of the physically impaired, Mike rode a wheelchair from Alaska to Washington, D.C. He often speaks in churches as advocate for the physically impaired. The following questions are ones which Mike could ask if you were considering ways to welcome people with certain special needs:

(1) Is there at least one primary entrance to the church facility which can be used by persons in wheelchairs?
(2) Do your doors have a clear opening of at least 32 inches? (Double doors must be operable by a single stroke or a handicapped person cannot use them.)
(3) Are toilet rooms accessible to handicapped, with a turning space of 60 by 60 inches to allow for wheelchair turning?
(4) Are water fountains easily hand-operated and accessible to people in wheelchairs?
(5) Are there seating spaces designated for the use of wheelchairs? (Perhaps a pew or two could be shortened.)

(6) Is transportation available for elderly or disabled people who don't drive?

(7) Do you invite persons with disabilities to have active roles in the worship service?

Making special efforts to provide access for new people can communicate a caring attitude and warm welcome. That way, if folks like Gordon and Joan are invited to a wedding at your church, they won't go home disappointed.

For Review, Study, and Action

(1) Have you had difficulty following directions to a place of worship? Tell about your experience. How do you help potential newcomers find your church?

(2) Take a look at your church sign, if you have one. What does its condition say about your church? How do you tell guests which door(s) to use to enter the building? Do you have signs on all the doors in the building?

(3) What might the condition of the building communicate to a first-time guest? How might you brighten the appearance of the building or make better use of your facilities?

(4) Take special notice of seating arrangements and where people sit during the worship service. Make a list of observations.

(5) Consider car parking. How might your church extend hospitality to the outside of your building?

(6) How do you provide for the care of babies and young children? What kind of welcome does your nursery facilities give to the younger generation?

(7) What kind of welcome does your church extend to people with special needs, such as the physically handicapped? How might you improve your welcome, as revealed by the checklist?

For Further Help

Accessibility Audit for Churches, edited by Toby Gould, Service Center, The United Methodist Church, 7820 Reading Road, Cincinnati, Ohio 45237. A helpful resource to help you measure the accessibility of your church facilities.

Mennonite Developmental Disability Services, Mennonite Central Committee, 21 South 21st St., Akron, Pa. 17501. This resource office can deal with specific questions or direct you to other agencies.

People Spots, by James Moss, Sr. (Eastern Pa. Conference Churches of God, 1988). Chapter five gives helpful information on seating patterns and seating capacity.

CHAPTER SEVEN

Saints Alive!

Our family once visited St. David's Cathedral in West Wales. This beautiful edifice houses the bones of the patron saint of Wales, along with the remains of other notable church leaders. As we walked through the huge sanctuary and chapels, we marveled at the magnificent windows and carved woodwork, the handiwork of skilled workers. It's an edifice dedicated to the glory of God.

However, there was a "dusty" feeling in the building. The atmosphere seemed like that of the Egyptian pyramids. St. David's is a memorial to what God did in the past. There are often more remains of departed saints in the building than bodies of living saints! Some churches seem similarly filled with stuffy saints. There is little life for new people to see and enjoy.

Stuffy Saints?

New Christians have a right to see the joy of the Lord in older Christians. Genuine joy doesn't mean, of course, pasting on an artificial smile just to make a good impression, or hiding problems. Genuine joy is the confidence of a relationship with Jesus Christ that endures even in difficult circumstances.

Several years ago, Mary Ellison lay in her upstairs

bedroom, dying of throat cancer. She radiated Christ's love even in the last stages of dying, when she could no longer speak. The nurses who attended her came downstairs weeping after being with her. The doctor, a nominal Christian, was so impressed by her radiance that he asked Mary's family for permission to bring his wife in to see her.

About the time Mary died, a young man across the street lost his father. He became manic-depressive. He let his beard and hair grow almost to his waist. Unable to escape his depression, he called on the doctor who had attended Mary Ellison.

The doctor told him, "I can give you drugs which will help you for three months or so. But if you go to that church over there [the Christian Center, where Mary had attended], they'll help you for the rest of your life."

With hope renewed, the young man began attending the church. Several weeks later, he made a decision to follow Christ. He enthusiastically helped the church with tract distribution. Shaking off the depression, he began regular Bible study with the pastor of the church. The prescription had worked!

Within a few months, ten additional people, from three different families, were attending the church as a result of this same doctor's recommendation. Mary Ellison reflected the joy of knowing Jesus, even on her deathbed. That kind of joy is contagious!

The Worship Service

Members of a church may be friendly and inviting, but without a vital spiritual life at the core of the congregation, new persons will be turned off. Oswald and Leas say it well:

No amount of propaganda or organization will cover a lack of substance at the core. It is folly for congregations to work at improving their incorporation process when they do not have substantial food to nourish people once they are incorporated. It's like putting whipped cream on stale pudding.[1]

New people can sense the strength of spiritual substance in a church during the worship hour. When people turn Godward in worship, they expose themselves at a deep level. And when they express themselves to one another, newcomers can sense the relational health of the church. By seeing saints that are alive and caring, new people soon sense God is alive among God's people. Consequently, the worship service is often the factor determining whether or not new people become part of the church.

People new to a church may not enjoy the same kind of worship long-term members enjoy. The worship style may serve as a barrier to receiving new members. Ray Bakke asserts that people are often so offended by thoughtless worship forms that they never have a real opportunity to be offended by the cross.[2] What kind of worship service will help a new believer worship in spirit and in truth—yet meet the needs of longtime members?

Dr. Peter Wilkes, pastor of South Hills Community Church (San Jose, Calif.) has pondered this question. For him, the incarnation of Christ is a basic biblical truth which should inform every aspect of the church's life. As Christ came into an alien world to identify with sinners, so must the church identify with the needs of those in the surrounding culture. This principle especially applies to welcoming new members into the local church.

Wilkes believes that most church activities should

aim to touch new people with the message of Jesus Christ. However, every sermon must somehow communicate with the broad spectrum of those in attendance. At South Hills, with about 2000 people present on a Sunday morning, this spectrum may include perhaps 10-20 percent who don't know Christ. There may be another 10 percent who are new Christians. A good number of Bible students may want a "meaty" Bible exposition. Then there will be a core group of regular church attenders who have heard the Word preached many times.

Obviously a congregation of 2000 struggles with different issues than a congregation of 50. Not everything Wilkes has learned will be applicable to those small congregations which far outnumber the giant ones. But one principle remains constant despite congregational size—the needs and backgrounds of church attenders can vary widely. Those congregations able to recognize and implement this understanding will be most skillful at creating a healthy blend of satisfied older members and excited newcomers.

Nowhere do tastes differ more than in music. Wilkes doesn't believe new attenders should have to endure a worship service whose music doesn't minister to unchurched people. So the congregation selects church music appealing to persons in contemporary culture. Peter believes that churches must adapt to a changing culture or be ineffective in making newcomers, particularly those who are new Christians, feel at home.

Robert came to Christ as a college student. Reflecting on his first church experience in a university town, he notes that the church music bore no resemblance to the music he personally enjoyed. Lacking the beat and rhythm, the drums and guitars and synthesizers he appreciated, it was, he had to confess, downright boring.

Because he sensed the truth and love embodied in the Christians whose fellowship he was enjoying, Robert endured the music. But he feels the poor music exemplifies needless barriers the church put in the way of his Christian growth.[3]

Robert was blessed to have a group of people who cared for him, even though the worship and music in the church seemed lackluster. Now he's a church musician, helping to enliven the worship services for others who are coming to Christ and the church.

Songs and poetry serve as reminders of people and the past. So for the older members, hymns are a rich repository of memories. But for new people unfamiliar with hymns, they have no such function.

It's said that people enjoy most the music they listened to as teenagers. This implies that in the church there are three different generations of musical preference. Unless the church makes an attempt to reach the musical tastes of more than one generation, some people will likely feel unable to worship from the heart.

Breaking Bread

Eating together is one of the most enjoyable and intimate activities people can share. In biblical times, eating had deep covenantal meanings. To eat with someone indicated fellowship and agreement. This is the background for the apostle Paul's command not to eat with a so-called church member whose life was drastically out of order (1 Cor. 5:11).

Communion is an expression of the covenant between God and God's people, through the mediation of Jesus Christ. Eating the covenant meal together is the most intimate expression of Christian fellowship. By breaking bread from house to house, the early church celebrated the presence of Christ. Every breaking of bread was a reminder of Christ. To welcome people to the communion table is to welcome them into Christ's fellowship. This is the ultimate welcome a church can give a new believer.

Some churches have found renewed meaning in communion through love feasts—eating a simple meal accompanied by sharing the emblematic bread and cup. Other churches encourage people to share communion in their homes or in small groups, for mutual spiritual encouragement.

Words That Communicate

A bishop in the Amish Mennonite Church told me about a struggle with changing the language of worship in his church. For years, the church had used only German in the worship services. He began to question this practice when members of the congregation invited friends who could not understand German to accompany them. On such occasions, the preacher spoke in English to accommodate the guests.

When non-German speaking guests became more frequent, the church made the switch to regular English services, with occasional German songs. They found it too difficult to prepare sermons in both languages, not knowing which they would use until the service began.

You may be saying to yourself, "I'm glad we don't have a language problem. Everyone can understand our service." Wait! Many people find it difficult to understand the words used in church, even if the language is English. Like a secret society, or a department within a university, a church can develop jargon that makes insiders feel *in* and outsiders *out*.

A church that wants to grow must use words readily understood by newcomers. A pastor who has helped several churches grow told me his method for testing the words he used in the service. As he prepared his sermon, he would think about a young couple who had just begun to attend church. They were new Christians unfamiliar with "churchy" language.

He kept asking himself, "Would Norman and Lisa understand these words and ideas?" As a result, he began to communicate more clearly. Surprisingly, older members of his church began complimenting him more on his sermons.

Have you ever noticed the simplicity with which Jesus spoke? He used few unfamiliar or long words. Yet his words attracted sinners as well as learned theologians. Juan Carlos Ortiz, a Latin evangelist, uses a simple formula—he tries to use language a twelve-year-old can understand. *Reader's Digest*, a magazine distributed around the world, is written at that level as well.

As times change, so does the language of the people. Consequently, the everyday language of the people in one generation sounds odd and outdated to another. Have you ever read a very old novel? If so, you surely found words and expressions which seemed quaint or foreign.

Many people likewise associate the King James Version of the Bible with castles or old churches with run-down graveyards. The language sounds like something King Arthur would have used to address his knights. Because we no longer use such language in ordinary conversation, it reminds people of the past. When the Scripture is read, it should give new Christians the feeling that God has something to communicate today. God is alive!

Furthermore, we can't assume that new people are familiar with the Bible. In a class I once taught for new members, one couple was having difficulty understanding how Moses and the Israelites could carry the ark of the covenant through the wilderness. They thought it was Noah's ark! I assured them that both arks had to do with a covenant, and their confusion needn't embarrass them.

A pastor's wife told about a woman who had joined their church. When the newcomer first attended, she had never heard of the crucifixion of Christ! The worship service or small-group Bible study should be a place where people can learn the basics without embarrassment.

When people are invited to turn to a biblical passage, we can give some description of where to find it, such as, "It's about halfway through the New Testament." Even if only one person benefits from such instruction, it's worth the effort. That person, feeling cared for, may invite others to come!

Alphabet Soup

In most denominations, or even congregations, there is some form of "alphabet soup." Abbreviations of the names of church commissions, committees, and service structures abound. In the Mennonite Church, for example, there are MCC, MDS, MBM, MCA, MMAA, MCLF, MEDA, MEEC, MMHS, MSEC, MRT, MWC, MPA, MYF, and MBCM, to name just a few. Noting the abundance of "M's," one new Hispanic Mennonite suggested perhaps it should be called the "M and M" church!

When such abbreviations are used in church life, new people are left groping. And having to ask for definitions simply increases a newcomer's sense of being an outsider. No one wants to seem stupid or ignorant, so it's easiest to remain silent. When it comes to asking questions, many newcomers reflect Abraham Lincoln's homespun philosophy: "It is better to remain silent and be thought a fool, than to speak up and remove all doubt."

The best way to make sure everyone understands announcements and messages is to use the full name of organizations, committees, or locations. This is true whenever you use abbreviations, whether written or spoken. Don't assume the reader or hearer knows what is being referred to, unless you have explained a reference previously.

Perhaps you're a church member who doesn't understand the language or words in the service. Or perhaps you're aware of others who don't understand the words or abbreviations. Why not compile a list of unfamiliar words or ideas used at your church and give them to the pastor?

Body Life

"It has been said that persons join a church for many reasons, but they stay for only one reason—relationships." The importance of relationships is stated most clearly in 1 Corinthians 12:12-27. Here Paul convincingly argues that in the church, all members (parts) have a vital role to play in the body of Christ, the church. No part is to be excluded. When one part suffers, every part suffers with it. The church is only as healthy as the relationship of its individual members to each other.

God combines the parts of the body in such a way that members have "equal concern for each other, in order that there should be no division in the body" (1 Cor. 12:25). With this kind of shared life, the chance of members "malfunctioning" or "being amputated" is greatly reduced.

Paul often refers to Christians' life together. In many of these references, he uses the words "one another," or "each other." A sampling of Paul's "one another" exhortations includes admonitions to instruct, build up, accept, encourage, serve, submit, and teach one another (see Rom. 15:7; 1 Cor. 14:12; 1 Thess. 4:18; Gal. 5:13; Eph. 5:21; and Col. 3:16).

The loving relationships Paul describes are not easily developed in the context of the large church fellowship which meets only once a week for worship. However, one can easily sense the strength of body life as it's expressed in the corporate worship service. Congregations that are alive and well have a spiritual dynamism. Their members pray for one another. They share joys and problems. They encourage one another through testimonies of God's power, provision, and love in their lives.

For Review, Study, and Action

(1) What comes to your mind when you hear the words "saints alive"?

(2) Discuss Peter Wilkes' idea that the incarnation of Christ can be a primary example of the way the church should relate to contemporary people. In what ways do you agree or disagree?

(3) Which generation do you suppose most enjoys the music in your worship service? How might the service be changed to appeal more readily to new Christians?

(4) Could a twelve-year-old understand the language of your worship service? In what ways could the service be adapted to help newcomers understand more easily what is said?

(5) Make a list of the "alphabet soup" letters used in your church. List expressions unique to your church.

(6) How does your church express body life?

(7) What is the best way to tell whether or not a person's commitment to Christ is genuine?

For Further Help

How to Build a Magnetic Church, by Herb Miller (Nashville: Abingdon Press, 1987). Chapter three outlines the elements needed for a vital worship service in today's society.

The Urban Christian: Effective Ministry in Today's Urban World, by Ray Bakke (Downers Grove: InterVarsity Press, 1987). This book by a well-known pastor and urbanologist is filled with practical examples of ways the church can adapt to the changing needs of society. It's especially helpful for urban congregations.

CHAPTER EIGHT

Welcome Mat

I was sitting in the departure lounge at Heathrow Airport in London. People of many descriptions and cultures walked by—young and old, punk rockers and business professionals, men with religious collars and women in saris, singles and couples, friends and relatives embracing those leaving. Seated behind me were several women in white saris, veiled except for their eyes. Around me were several bearded men with turbans, conversing in a foreign tongue.

Suddenly, the men stood up and pushed apart the two sets of lounge chairs. They removed their shoes. An energetic old man with a gray beard pulled a folded cloth from his travel bag and spread it on the floor in front of us. Five men seated themselves in a tight circle on the cloth, jovially conversing and making preparations for a meal. One man produced a bright red water pitcher with a spout. Another uncovered a plastic container filled with ground meat. A third laid out a stack of thin cakes.

The man sitting opposite me on the lounge chair had no room to sit in the circle on the floor, so he remained in his chair. He glanced at me and invited me in broken English, "Will you join us for meat?"

At first I was taken aback. Then I graciously declined, having just finished lunch. But I observed with interest as the men quickly ate. They tore off pieces of the flat cakes and dipped them into the meat dish. In just a few minutes, the bowl of meat was empty, the uneaten cakes were put into a plastic bag, and the cloth was folded up and put away. The men wiped their hands on their flowing robes and returned the lounge furniture to its place. Soon afterward, they all left to board their plane.

These strangers (identified by their flight bags as Pakistanis) offered me hospitality. One of the men wore a specially designed skull cap, presumably Islamic. These people of another faith reached out to me, a stranger. Would I have offered such hospitality to them? Would you have?

A Rose by Any Other Name . . .?

How do you refer to people who are visiting your church for the first time? Are they *strangers*? *Visitors*? *Guests*? More than once, I've heard someone say from a pulpit, "I see we have some strange faces with us today." Although I knew what was meant, it gave me a creepy feeling to think of guests with strange-looking faces. What do your words of welcome say to guests?

The Ministry of Hospitality

The spread of the early church is linked to the fellowship of believers meeting in homes. There is no mention in the New Testament of buildings designed for Christian worship. In fact, there is little evidence to show that there *were* Christian meetinghouses in the first two centuries following Pentecost. Instead, as persons became Christians, they were welcomed into house fellowships. People opened their homes for worship and fellowship.

Some of the hosts mentioned in the Scripture are Aquila and Priscilla (1 Cor. 16:19); Philemon (Philem. 1-2); Lydia (Acts 16:14-15); and Mary (Acts 12:12). Meeting in homes, people developed relationships with friends and shared the good news. In this context, people not only heard about the love of Jesus; they experienced it. The power of love was demonstrated in the ministry of listening, caring, and sharing.

As in those early days, hospitality is one of the most important ministries of the church today. Without the gracious hospitality of individuals and groups in the church, new persons won't be attracted to the church. There is no evangelistic substitute for the love of God ministered by the body of Christ. Jesus said it this way: "Everyone will know that you are my disciples if you love one another" (John 13:35).

The ministry of hospitality mustn't be confused with the art of entertainment. Many guests simply want to be loved and accepted, not impressed. In fact, new people may feel uncomfortable if they sense the host is trying to impress them. When this happens, the host, not the guest, becomes the focus of attention.

Putting Your Best Foot Forward

Congregations formally greet guests in various ways. Some have greeters who stand at the doors each Sunday, shaking hands with worshipers as they enter. Other churches designate "host families" who greet people as they enter and invite church visitors home to lunch. Still others have hosts standing by a guest register, where visitors may write their names.

A greeter is to a church what a receptionist is to a business or social organization. This is a good place to put the best foot forward. Some people have a natural ability to welcome people and make them feel at home.

Others exercise the spiritual gifts of encouragement and mercy. These are the people who can serve exceptionally well as greeters.

Good greeters soon develop an "eagle eye" for newcomers, especially if the church isn't too large. They can spot guests and help them with any needs. When visitors come unaccompanied by anyone from the church, the greeter can quickly introduce them to someone who can make them feel at home.

One large congregation in Pennsylvania has greeters or ushers at several different places around the facility. Each outside entrance door or inside "directional change point" has someone who can help newcomers. This same church has discovered that it's helpful to have the greeter stand outside, rather than inside, the entrance doors. This symbolizes that the church is taking the first step toward the guest.

Greeting One Another

In many cases, a welcome by a formal greeter is less effective than informal greetings from other interested people. Five times in the New Testament, people in the churches are encouraged to greet one another (see Rom. 16:16; 1 Cor. 16:20; 2 Cor. 13:12; 1 Thess. 5:26; 1 Pet. 5:14). Some are told to greet one another with a holy kiss, or a kiss of love.

Why do the biblical writers emphasize this? Perhaps because a greeting is a form of acknowledgment, a way of recognizing worth in another. To visit a congregation and not be acknowledged is painful.

It's important to greet people we don't know. Jesus taught his disciples:

> If you love those who love you, what reward will you get? Are not even the tax collectors doing that? And if

you greet only your brothers, what are you doing more than others? Do not even pagans do that? Be perfect, therefore, as your heavenly Father is perfect" (Matt. 5:46-48).

A good time to help people greet others is during the service. At a specified time, everyone can be encouraged to reach out and greet people around them. In this way, most people will touch several others with warmth and welcome.

At Cedar Mill Bible Church, pastoral leaders Al and Roberta Wollen exemplified hospitality for years. God blessed their efforts, and over 35 years they saw the congregation grow many times over. Every Sunday, Al led the people in greeting one another during the service. From the pulpit, he emphasized the importance of greeting guests. As a result, people begin to naturally greet guests. One 16-year-old boy told Al he had been greeted 16 times in one service!

Introducing Guests

There are many ways to introduce guests in a worship service. Not all guests like to be introduced in the same way. Some enjoy being introduced publicly in the worship service. They may be offended if not so recognized. They may be former members who moved away and have come back to visit. Or they may be relatives of people in the church. They will gladly stand when their names are called and acknowledge the welcome.

Most people, however, prefer not to be named in public. They may blush with embarrassment if their names are called or they are asked to stand. For whatever reason, they don't want too much attention focused on them.

How can a church show proper sensitivity in introducing all types of people? One possibility is to ask guests how they want to be introduced. To consistently follow this practice, the church has to find ways to ask the guest before introduction time. Some churches use a guest register or pew cards which can be used for this purpose. A greeter or host can also get the information.

Particularly in larger congregations, it may be best to simply have everyone greet the people around them. Although guests aren't specially recognized by the whole congregation, they are recognized by those sitting close by. The pastor can extend a warm welcome to all guests. The worship bulletin can also have a special note of welcome to guests.

Folding People into the Church

South Hills Community Church reaches out in a special way to newcomers. Each Sunday morning, the worship leader welcomes the visitors. Pastor Peter Wilkes gives a brief instruction to first-time visitors, then ushers hand out an attractive four-color brochure about the church.

Included in the packet is a visitor card. About 60 percent of those who take the brochure return a completed visitor card. These persons are then invited to a once-monthly dinner with other recent church visitors, along with the pastor. (Persons are given three invitations, in case of schedule conflicts or initial reluctance to attend.) After the meal, Wilkes explains the church's philosophy of ministry and how newcomers can become involved in the life of the church.

Once each month, the church shares communion. In preparation for sharing together, Wilkes explains the meaning of communion. Noting that the sharing of communion is for believers, he invites non-Christians to make a commitment to Christ in the service. He leads respondents in a prayer of commitment to Christ. He then invites these new believers to share communion with the older believers.

The church slogan is "We are a people church." Wilkes emphasizes the importance of welcoming new people. He tries to model and teach hospitality. For example, when he sees a person standing without a hymnbook in the worship service, he offers one, with the book open to the proper page number. He insists that this kind of modeling is essential to teach hospitality to others in the church.

Follow-up for Guests

One form of hospitality is to be in touch with your guests shortly after their visit to your congregation. (In chapter twelve I look at a good way to get their names and addresses.) It's common for pastors to send a letter to first-time guests. This demonstrates goodwill.

The best follow-up, however, seems to be a visit to the guest's home. Herb Miller notes:

> When laypersons make fifteen-minute visits to the homes of first time worship visitors within thirty-six hours, 85 percent of them return the following week. Make this home visit within seventy-two hours, and 60 percent of them will return. Make it seven days later, and 15 percent will return. The pastor making this call, rather than laypersons, cuts each result in half.[1]

When the pastor calls, it can be perceived as an obligation. But if members of the church call, it communicates a genuine interest on the part of the church.

Pastor Ken Nauman from Ashton, Florida, has seen his church grow through the use of a visitation program named Night of Caring. This program trains members of the congregation to call on worship visitors regularly. They have learned to extend the love of Christ in a caring home visit.

How does your congregation show your worship guests that you want them to return? Prompt and caring follow-up will go a long way.

For Review, Study, and Action

(1) Review the story of the foreigners at the first part of the chapter. Would you have eaten with them? Would you have offered to share your lunch with them?

(2) How do you refer to visitors in your worship service? Discuss the implications of the various words that could be used to designate visitors.

(3) Discuss the relationship between hospitality and church growth in the days of the early church. How is hospitality linked to church growth today?

(4) What are the differences between hospitality shown by a congregation and hospitality in the home? Who is responsible to see that the church is showing hospitality?

(5) How does your church greet guests? Do you favor having formal greeters or informal greetings? How do you put your best foot forward as a church?

(6) Discuss the biblical teaching about greeting one another. How do people in your church greet one another?

(7) How do you introduce guests in your Sunday worship service? In what ways might you improve your introductions?

(8) How do you fold new people into your congregation? What kind of follow-up do you have for guests in the worship service?

(9) How do you let people know what your church is all about?

For Further Help

How to Build a Magnetic Church, by Herb Miller (Nashville: Abingdon Press, 1987). Chapter six has helpful advice on visiting the visitors to your church. Miller gives helpful ideas for both training and implementation.

Night of Caring, a video series available from Dynamic Communications, 127 North Madison Ave., Suite 22, Pasadena, Calif. 91101. The set humorously illustrates "do's and don'ts" of visitation.

Open Heart, Open Home, by Karen Burton Mains (Elgin: David C. Cook, 1976). The author shows how to develop a hospitable approach to others, sharing from her own personal experience.

CHAPTER NINE

Open Arms

Two of Kenmore and Regina's children were born with cleft palates. The second of the two was born with a severe case. When the baby was ready to leave the hospital, the doctor asked whether the parents wanted to take the baby home or leave him in the state's care. Kenmore and Regina were surprised he would ask such a question. The doctor explained that some parents choose not to keep this kind of child. For Kenmore's family, this was unthinkable. They were confident that they could care for the child. They loved him and wouldn't think of giving him up.

The son is now grown. He had five surgical operations to correct his condition. Since he wears a mustache, one can hardly notice he ever had a cleft palate.

Upon reflection, Kenmore believes this is a parable of the church. There are times God sends seemingly undesirable new children to the church. The church may reject them, choosing to let someone else care for them. But new Christians can grow and mature until one is proud they are part of the family. What a loss it would be to not have them!

Closed Doors

The story is told of a man who walked the streets of a large city one Sunday morning, looking for a place to worship. He found a church whose services appealed to him. But the ushers refused to let him enter because his skin was the wrong color. Dejected, he sat on the pavement outside. Soon, a stranger came and asked what was wrong. He poured out his feelings of rejection. The man comforted him, saying, "That's okay. They wouldn't let me in either." As the stranger faded away, the rejected man realized it was Jesus who had appeared to him.

People have long rejected the very person or God they claim to worship. In Jesus' day, there were two places of public worship for Jewish people—the temple in Jerusalem and the synagogues in various towns or cities. The men in charge of worship were called synagogue rulers, scribes, or priests. The high priest and the Sanhedrin (which functioned like a religious parliament) had primary control of spiritual life. They enforced the rules for fitting into the religious system.

Jesus clashed with these leaders, especially the Pharisees.

> . . . you nullify the word of God for the sake of your tradition. You hypocrites! Isaiah was right when he prophesied about you: "These people honor me with their lips, but their hearts are far from me. They worship me in vain; their teachings are but rules taught by men" (Matt. 15:6-9).

The traditions and teachings of the Pharisees, originally intended as guidelines to help persons obey the law, had turned into a law themselves. Now, in effect, they worshiped their own law instead of the God they claimed to worship.

"You shut the kingdom of heaven in people's faces," Jesus accused the religious leaders. "You yourselves do not enter, nor will you let those enter who are trying to" (Matt. 23:13-14; Luke 11:52). The leaders, appointed as guardians of the door to life, were refusing to enter themselves.

They were also blocking the way for others. Lepers, prostitutes, tax collectors, countless needy people who couldn't meet the rigid Pharisaic law—all were excluded. How tragic! The gatekeepers had replaced the door to salvation with an impenetrable wall.

Was it that these people wanted no converts? No. Jesus went on to say, "You travel over land and sea to win a single convert, and when he becomes one, you make him twice as much a son of hell as you are" (Matt. 23:15).

Apparently they made heroic efforts to make new converts. But they would accept only those willing to conform to all prescribed laws and customs. By forcing these would-be believers into the same legalistic mold they had made for themselves, they pushed them away from the kingdom of heaven.

Could a similar tragedy happen in the church today? Yes, new people have come to a church only to discover that tradition and rules have replaced genuine worship of God. When this is true, new people are the first to feel it and be excluded, since they don't fit into the religious system. Genuine worship introduces people to God without demanding legalistic conformity to a set of rules.

Some of the saddest words in Scripture were written by the apostle John.

The true light that gives light to every man was coming into the world. He was in the world, and though the world was made through him, the world did not recognize him. He came to that which was his own, but his own did not receive him (John 1:9-11).

Sometimes Jesus was refused hospitality even by those who professed to believe in him. He said to the church at Laodicea, "Here I am! I stand at the door and knock. If anyone hears my voice and opens the door, I will go in and eat with him, and he with me" (Rev. 3:20). These words are sometimes used to represent Jesus seeking entrance to a sinner's heart. Perhaps that's an appropriate application. But the words were spoken to a church! Apparently church members were blocking Jesus from their lives because they didn't think they needed him. They thought they were doing well enough without him.

People who haven't received Jesus into their own lives can't genuinely welcome others in Jesus' name. It is Jesus himself who makes it possible for us to receive others from the heart, even though they may have a different skin color, think differently, or wear clothing that seems strange to us.

Guidelines for Invitations

While at the home of a prominent Pharisee, Jesus noticed how the guests picked the best seats. He told a parable to teach the importance of humility (see Luke 14:7-11). Jesus gave a radical solution to the problem of playing favorites. He said:

> When you give a luncheon or dinner, do not invite your friends, your brothers or relatives, or your rich neighbors; if you do, they may invite you back and so you will be repaid. But when you give a banquet, invite the poor, the crippled, the lame, the blind, and you will be blessed. Although they cannot repay you, you will be

repaid at the resurrection of the righteous, (Luke 14:12-14).

In his letter to Christians, the elder James wrote:

> . . . as believers in our glorious Lord Jesus Christ, don't show favoritism. Suppose a man comes into your meeting wearing a gold ring and fine clothes, and a poor man in shabby clothes also comes in. If you show special attention to the man wearing fine clothes and say, "Here's a good seat for you," but say to the poor man, "You stand there," or "Sit on the floor by my feet," have you not discriminated among yourselves and become judges with evil thoughts?
> If you really keep the royal law found in Scripture, "Love your neighbor as yourself," you are doing right. But if you show favoritism, you sin and are convicted by the law as lawbreakers (James 2:1-4, 8-9).

Most of us enjoy being with people we respect. Given a choice between a needy new member or someone who is resourceful, we often choose the latter. But the Scriptures warn against showing hospitality only to those who meet our criteria for respect.

The apostle Peter learned this lesson some years after he came to faith. Through a vision, God sent him to the household of Cornelius, a Roman centurion. According to Jewish teaching, Peter shouldn't have entered the man's house. But the Spirit prompted him to do so. When he saw the gathered group, he said, "I now realize how true it is that God does not show favoritism but accepts men from every nation who fear him and do what is right" (Acts 10:34-35).

Peter had probably known this truth in some measure earlier. But coming face-to-face with eager inquirers helped the truth sink in. Now he not only knew but experienced the truth. The same can happen to us as we learn to know new believers personally. We'll experience for ourselves the joy of seeing how God welcomes people into the family.

Genuine Acceptance

Jesus consistently accepted and loved people others rejected. Most memorable is the incident of a woman he loved despite the scandal it caused. A sinful woman approached Jesus while he ate with Simon the Pharisee, and anointed his feet with perfume and her tears (Luke 7:36-38). Jesus told Simon,

> "Do you see this woman? I came into your house. You did not give me any water for my feet, but she wet my feet with her tears and wiped them with her hair. You did not give me a kiss, but this woman, from the time I entered, has not stopped kissing my feet. You did not put oil on my head, but she has poured perfume on my feet. Therefore, I tell you, her many sins have been forgiven—for she loved much. But he who has been forgiven little loves little." (Luke 7:44-47)

Simon, the host, hadn't provided even the basic courtesies. Perhaps he didn't want to appear too hospitable, since Jesus was a controversial figure. But the woman ministered to Jesus. Simon had grudgingly given him a place in his home. Her tears, kisses, and perfume showed she had given Jesus a place in her heart. There is a vital difference.

A church may provide a formal greeting and warm handshake, but these alone won't draw people into fellowship. People must sense a welcome from the heart.

Ray Stedman tells of an incident which took place at the Peninsula Bible Church. While preaching, Stedman had read 1 Corinthians 6:9-11, which gives a long list of sins, then promises God through Jesus can cleanse us from such sin.

On an impulse, Stedman decided to ask people to stand if they had been redeemed by Christ from any of the sins mentioned. There was a long pause. No one moved. Finally, a frail old woman stood. Then several others stood. After a time, people all over the congregation were standing. Ray thanked them for their honesty and openness and thanked God for cleansing their sin.

Later, Ray discovered that a young man who wasn't a Christian had been in the congregation. Never having been in church before, he was "nervous as a cat." He told Ray that when he saw all those people standing to admit that they were saved by God's grace from all those sins, he relaxed and thought to himself, "These are my kind of people!" As a result, he committed his life to Jesus Christ!

Regardless of the nature of our sins, we can be saved only by the power of Jesus Christ. There is no room for pride or boasting which excludes others as not good enough to belong to our group. Nevertheless, from the time of the apostles, the faithful church has struggled to determine the grounds for full acceptance into the congregation. The way the early church dealt with the matter can be helpful to us today.

Spiritual Barriers to Acceptance

After a period of rapid growth and the commissioning of two missionaries, the multiethnic congregation at Antioch was feeling the strain of divided loyalties. Paul and Barnabas, the cofounders of the church, were being challenged by teachers from the "home church" in Jerusalem. These self-appointed instructors were declaring, "Unless you are circumcised according to the custom taught by Moses, you cannot be saved" (Acts 15:1).

This challenge distressed the new believers and brought Paul and Barnabas into sharp dispute with the guest teachers. At that time, circumcision was universally understood as the distinguishing mark of a Jew. Gentile converts who refused to be circumcised seemed to be rejecting the Jewish faith and the Scriptures. This was unthinkable for persons whose Jewish roots were a vital part of their spiritual life.

Since the issue couldn't be resolved on a local level, Paul and Barnabas were appointed, along with others, to consult with the apostles and elders at Jerusalem. The foremost church authorities carefully considered this controversial issue.

In short, it was a question of how the Gentile converts could be received into the predominately Jewish group of believers. Would new Gentile believers need to become practicing Jews? Or could they worship God by simply following the way of Jesus Christ?

In a landmark decision, the Jerusalem church decided that the Gentile Christians could be believers in their own right (see Acts 15:1-35). They didn't need to become Jews or keep the law of Moses. The convention issued a letter to be sent to all the churches. It notified them of the official decision and indicated that the Holy Spirit had played a key role.

Even so, Paul battled for years with the Judaizers (strict Jewish teachers), determined to persuade new Gentile Christians to keep Jewish laws. Paul makes many references to this problem in his letters to new churches (see 1 Cor. 7:17-20; Rom. 4:9-12; Gal. 2:11-16; 5:1-12; Phil. 3:2-4).

In addition to circumcision, some churches were divided on matters of lesser importance. Believers in the churches at Rome and Corinth were accustomed to buying meat formerly offered to idols as part of the worship ritual in an idol's temple. The meat was sold at bargain prices, and frugal Christians were taking advantage of the savings.

Some new believers, just converted from a life of idol worship, found this practice threatening to their newfound faith in Christ. They spoke against the practice, apparently accusing others of idolatry. They knew that if they themselves frequented the idol temples, they might well be pulled back into their old way of life. For this reason, Paul referred to them as "the weak." He urged the mature Christians to "accept him whose faith is weak, without passing judgment on disputable matters" (Rom. 14:1).

Paul urged the stronger persons to demonstrate love, rather than engage in rational arguments.

> Now about food sacrificed to idols: We know that we all possess knowledge. Knowledge puffs up, but love builds up. The man who thinks he knows something does not yet know as he ought to know. But the man who loves God is known by God (1 Cor. 8:1-3).

Paul understood that love would be the only adequate solution to this difficult problem. His approach to such disputes is summed up in the saying, "Accept one another, then, just as Christ accepted you, in order to bring praise to God" (Rom. 15:7). To accept one another means to recognize that the other is part of the body of Christ, even though there may be disagreement on matters not basic to salvation.

Tragically, new Christians rejected by someone in the church sometimes become discouraged and return to a life of sin. Love compels us to accept those who have named Jesus as Lord. We mustn't reject them because we disagree on matters of doctrine not basic to salvation.

Growing, maturing churches maintain a careful balance between Christian freedom and strict adherence to rules or tradition. The former may cause compromise of Christian principles. The latter may lead to legalistic bondage.

New Christians coming into the church can help older Christians experience the freshness of a new commitment to Christ. Older Christians can help provide guidelines for faithful obedience. When a spirit of mutual acceptance prevails, the atmosphere is ripe for sustained Christian growth.

Understanding the Feelings of New People

It was the custom in my boyhood church for the pastor to ask a committed layperson to pray publicly without advance notice. On one occasion, the pastor called the congregation to prayer, and asked Fred to lead. He was referring to a middle-aged gentleman who was an adult Sunday school teacher and a committed member.

That Sunday, another man named Fred, who rarely attended any church, was a guest. When he heard his name, panic crossed his face. The pastor soon noticed and clarified which "Fred" he had intended. But that look of panic is etched on my memory.

Although your church might not call on a member of the congregation to pray, the unchurched guest may still be on edge, not knowing what will be expected.

The unchurched or very irregular attenders may feel uncomfortable and uneasy for a variety of reasons. They may feel conspicuous and out of place, because the church is foreign environment to them. They may fear being laughed at by unchurched people who discover they have been to church. They may fear being asked to read Scripture or pray aloud. How does your church help put new people at ease?

For Review, Study, and Action

(1) Read Revelation 3:14-22. What do you suppose Jesus meant when he said he stands at the door and knocks? Was he speaking to the fellowship as a whole or individual members? What might he be saying to your fellowship?

(2) What kind of person might your fellowship be most reluctant to accept? What kind of person is most readily received?

(3) Discuss the relationship between hospitality in the home and in the heart.

(4) Discuss spiritual barriers to acceptance. What issues in your church are similar to the issue of circumcision in early Christian times?

(5) Can you think of an occasion when a weak brother or sister was caused to stumble by lack of acceptance and understanding? Share any helpful insights.

(6) What kind of acceptance have you experienced when visiting other churches? Share any helpful insights gained from your experiences.

(7) Make a list of new people who have come to your church in the past six months. What feelings might they have? Has anyone lent a listening ear regarding the events that preceded their coming to your church?

For Further Help

Creating Communities of the Kingdom, by David W. Shenk and Ervin R. Stutzman (Scottdale: Herald Press, 1988). Chapters seven and eight give guidelines for dealing with questions of cultural differences in the congregation.

Key to a Loving Heart, by Karen Burton Mains (Elgin: David C. Cook, 1979). The author shows how the love and forgiveness of Christ helps us open our hearts to others.

A World of Difference, by Thom Hopler (Downers Grove: InterVarsity Press, 1981). This is a delightful description of cultural differences and how these differences affect a people's perception of the gospel.

CHAPTER TEN

Fitting In

Mervin Deiter is a stonemason in much demand because of his excellent work. I enjoy watching him build or repair stone walls. He fits each stone into place, making a unique pattern. Small stones, large stones, odd-shaped stones—all are arranged together to form a strong wall.

The Scripture says: ". . . you also, like living stones, are being built into a spiritual house to be a holy priesthood . . ." (1 Pet. 2:5). Other Bible verses also emphasize this idea.

> . . . you are . . . built on the foundation of the apostles and prophets, with Christ Jesus himself as the chief cornerstone. In him the whole building is joined together and rises to become a holy temple in the Lord. And in him you too are being built together to become a dwelling in which God lives by his Spirit (Eph. 2:19-22).

> . . . you are . . . God's building (1 Cor. 3:9).

Loose stones lying on a pile or scattered on the ground are easily stolen or moved around. But stones cemented into the wall of a house are more permanent.

The apostle Paul used yet another word picture to describe the relationship of Christians to one another.

"Now you are the body of Christ, and each one of you is a part of it" (1 Cor. 12:27).

Paul emphasized the vital contribution each makes to the whole body.

> . . . God has arranged the parts in the body, every one of them, just as he wanted them to be. If they were all one part, where would the body be? As it is, there are many parts, but one body." (1 Cor. 12:18-20)

Both word pictures portray organization and structure. The stones, as well as the body parts, have to do with the contribution of a single part to the formation of the whole. The building metaphor portrays *security*, a place of protection and belonging in the structure. The body metaphor portrays *belonging* as well as *significance*.

Life flows through each of the church's parts. But without proper organization, that life would cease. Cancer illustrates disorder's effects. It represents a breakdown of proper function and organization.

How can the church provide security of belonging and significance of ministry for each person in the church? How can the church help new people fit into the structure so they find a place of fellowship and ministry? These are questions I'll address in the rest of this chapter.

Small Groups in the Church

Small groups of Christians have been meeting since Pentecost, with varying purposes. The churches which received Paul's original letters met in homes and shared the Epistles with other house fellowships. The members of the church were intimately involved in one another's lives.

The Wesleyan class meetings were small-group fellowships. These meetings led to the establishment of the Methodist Church, so named because of the methodical way people and programs were organized for nurture. For 100 years, to be a Methodist was to belong to a small group. People attended church Sunday morning and class meeting Sunday night.

Today, the church in Asia leads the way in small-group formation. The world-renowned Korean church, led by Paul Cho, thrives through the ministry of small groups. The church in China has also been growing spectacularly in the past decade, even under oppression, through small groups.

Most satisfied church members identify with some subgroup within the church—a Sunday school class, a committee, a special-interest group, or a home group. Effective small groups help meet the needs of newer members and stimulate congregational life. Following are several principles regarding the role of small groups in the church. Small groups help participants:

(1) Develop meaningful relationships among the group members.
(2) Study the Scriptures and make meaningful applications to life.
(3) Minister to others beyond the group.

A weekly group meeting may be the most effective way of accomplishing the above objectives. Groups which meet less often tend to be less effective. In order to really encourage each other in discipleship, group members need to know one another's working lives and home lives, as well as their church lives.

Bible study is an important focus for a small group. New groups might begin by studying the Gospel of

Mark, then the Gospel of John, followed by the first epistle of John. After that, any New Testament book could be used (although Hebrews and Revelation should be studied only after a thorough familiarity with the Old Testament). *The NIV Serendipity Bible for Study Groups* can be a very helpful tool for small-group Bible study.

As Christians submit themselves to the authority of the Scriptures, the Holy Spirit convicts of sin, of righteousness, and of judgment. A great hindrance to church growth is a lack of genuine repentance among professing Christians. Adult Bible study groups can tend to become subject-oriented or teacher-oriented.

This leads to a weakness in two areas. First, there is little interpersonal ministry among participants. Second, there is little evangelism taking place. Small groups that focus on practical application of Scripture can help avoid these tendencies.

Church leaders must take responsibility to supervise and train small-group leaders. Small-group leaders can benefit from regular meetings with the pastor or other church leaders. They can encourage one another and work through problems. They can also determine the study materials for small groups. Twice-yearly training sessions can keep leaders on the growing edge and help produce new leaders. New groups can then be formed at least twice a year.

New groups tend to incorporate newcomers more easily than older groups. When a group first begins, everyone is on equal ground in terms of the group's history and experience. The fellowship may be shallow. But it is inclusive.

As the group ages, the fellowship deepens. But the group becomes more exclusive. A newcomer may feel awkward breaking into a series of discussions, or not understanding the group's way of doing things.

The greater the diversity in group life, the greater the growth potential of the church. Because different groups meet different needs, many different people can have their needs met. When more needs are being met, the church is more likely to attract new people. For example, junior and senior high school groups have different needs. If there are separate groups for these rapidly changing adolescents, they are more likely to invite their friends.

A single-cell church may prefer to be one big happy family. But even a family will break into separate interest groups. There aren't many activities which keep three generations interested for long periods of time.

At an extended family reunion, for example, there may be several clusters of small groups. The children may go to a playground or a nearby park. One group may be clustered around Grandmother's latest craft project. Another may be in the garden, examining the homeowner's plans for a new patio extension. Still another may be crowded in the living room, watching a video or catching a sports show.

All groups have a saturation point. It may be because someone's living room seats only twelve people, or because three people tend to do all the talking. For whatever reason, groups reach a point at which they won't easily grow. As groups near saturation, they find it less easy to incorporate someone new.

Sensitivity in introducing the concept of small groups is essential. Some churches strongly resist small-group development. This tends to be true of rural churches and those with many blood ties in the church fellowship. It's best not to push such people into groups. Small groups can instead be offered for those who want them.

Some people aren't prepared to deal with the potential intimacy of a small group. Perhaps they have just experienced hurt and are feeling vulnerable. Or perhaps they have been taught that small groups are wrong. (Some churches have specifically forbidden small-group meetings.) Again, they may simply be shy and reserved and just need private space.

The Effect of Church Size

A church's capacity to grow is directly related to its structure. Leadership structure becomes more crucial as a church grows, because it takes more energy and administration to keep a large church growing. It can't easily use the same decision-making process as a small church.

Large churches tend to put major decisions in the hands of a few capable people. For example, there is one large, growing church that has only one committee—a property committee. But the people in this church are involved in many ministries—many of them in community-oriented services. Large churches usually give more *authority* to a few. They then give more *ministry opportunities* to many.

A church that is trying to improve its welcome will need to consider the dynamics of church size. What works for a large urban church may not work for a small rural church. Likewise, a pastor who has successfully used a particular approach in one parish may be disappointed to find it doesn't work in another.

Each church size poses unique problems for receiving new members. The examples in this book have been drawn from churches of all sizes. Readers will need to discern which insights are most appropriate for a particular situation.

Below I'll discuss three general categories of church

size, along with implications for incorporating new people.

The small church. Small churches function like a family. When people are welcomed into a small church, they become an integral part of the family. There are jobs for everyone. Small churches are good places for people to develop their gifts and abilities. Everyone's contribution is valued.

Small churches sometimes include several nuclear or extended families. A member of one of these families may be a "gatekeeper." If the gatekeeper rejects a newcomer, the rest of the fellowship may follow suit.

Even new pastors may feel excluded by a small, single-celled church. They may find it difficult to function effectively. Many small churches can't afford a full-time pastor. In these churches, most program direction and decision-making power is held by laypeople.

Receiving a new member in the small church is much like adopting a child. Since fitting into a family takes time, it may take several years for a new person to really feel at home. Spouses of church members tend to find it easiest to fit quickly into the church. In a way, they "marry into the church."

The medium-sized church. As church size increases, there are growing professional expectations of the pastor. The pastor may "run the church" and try to be involved in all aspects of church life. The pastor may be expected to do everything, including evangelistic outreach. Consequently, newcomers may be attracted to the ministry of the pastor, who becomes the primary "magnet" attracting people to the church.

The pastor also becomes an important factor in whether or not people feel incorporated into the church. Growth through conversion in this size church may easily be "choked out" by a pastor's lack of time to keep meeting new people.

As a church grows beyond the ability of a pastor to know and care for each individual, one of two things will likely happen. The church will stop growing. Or the pastor will find other ways to provide for pastoral oversight. Single-pastor churches tend to plateau in attendance at about 200. This figure seems to represent the number of people which can be pastored by one person.

It may be difficult for a newcomer to find a place of belonging in a medium-sized church, particularly if there is no small-group structure. It's hard to belong to a group of 100-300 people. Unless they find their needs met in a small group, new people may leave through the back door.

The large church. The large church may well contain several small "churches." Members may not know everyone in the whole church. But they can know everyone in their Sunday school class or other small group.

Newcomers are often received into one of the smaller groups first. They join the church later. Consequently, there may be more than one stage of joining. The pastor may have only passing acquaintance with many members. It's impossible to personally know hundreds of people. And the pastor's time is likely to be consumed with administrative oversight and committee meetings.

Particularly for large churches, the rancher motif for pastoral care seems more applicable than the shepherd motif. The rancher works through shepherds, who in turn provide personal pastoral care. Pastoral care is multiplied by working with "flocks within a flock."

New people who visit the church can easily be missed unless there is a careful follow-up system. New people need an invitation to small groups and also to worship services. Leaders train and equip, so that members can feel significant and find a place of ministry in the church or community.

Every Member Is a Minister

Mount Joy Mennonite Church in Pennsylvania has the slogan: ". . . where every member is a minister. . ." The idea comes from 1 Peter: "You are . . . a royal priesthood"(2:9), and Ephesians: "It is he [Christ] who gave . . . apostles, . . . prophets, . . . evangelists, . . . pastors and teachers to *prepare God's people for works of service. . . .*" The church will be strengthened "*as each part does its work*" (4:11-12, 16, italics added).

There is harmony and growth in the body of Christ when all find the places of ministry which fit their gifts. A positive approach is to "employ" each church member according to his or her spiritual gift(s), as Peter urged. "Each one should use whatever gift he has received to serve others, faithfully administering God's grace in its various forms" (1 Pet. 4:10).

Meaningful Work

Most church workers are volunteers or unpaid helpers. Perhaps they are "draftees," who serve out of a sense of obligation or duty. Churches usually recruit in one of five ways. In order of frequency, they are:

(1) Bulletin board or newsletter announcement
(2) Pulpit announcement
(3) Letter
(4) Phone call
(5) Face-to-face contact

Experience and research show these are in inverse order of effectiveness![1] By making a face-to-face appeal, you communicate the significance and importance of the task. Reticent or shy people need such encouragement to become involved. Many newcomers are eager to serve. They will make significant contributions if properly approached.

Since new people haven't been worn out by past service, they may accept roles more easily than long-term members. "Under-employed" members will often drop out of the church fellowship because they don't feel they're making a significant contribution. Eager new members should find a place of ministry within the first year. Persons properly suited for their jobs will be fulfilled and won't readily leave the church.

On the other hand, some newcomers may be overwhelmed if asked to serve too soon. They may need a time of discipleship and personal caring to equip them for service.

I was once mistakenly introduced to a group of pastors as coauthor of a book entitled *Creating Committees of the Kingdom*. The man who introduced me had misread the prompt sheet to say "committees" instead of "communities." I shuddered. I was sure most of the pastors in that group didn't want to hear about committees. Somehow, committees and kingdom don't seem to go together. Nevertheless, most churches use committees to accomplish the work of the church.

Can committees really be agencies of God's kingdom? Surely—but only 20 percent of an average congregation will enjoy committee work. The rest would rather fulfill a task. Consequently, committee people need to be carefully selected.

Making Expectations Clear

Many people refuse to take jobs within the church for fear of failure. Whether in the business world or in the church, people feel best about taking on a task or role when they know they can do it properly. They don't like fuzzy guidelines like "Oh, anybody can do it," or "We'll tell you if you do something wrong."

Clear job descriptions, or "ministry descriptions," can be a vital asset to new people taking on a new task. Putting something on paper will clarify the task for everyone, including the person asked to do the job. It's a simple way to clarify assumptions and expectations.

New Christians are particularly sensitive to expectations. They may be easily hurt when told to do a job only to discover people are dissatisfied. It's far better to clarify expectations at the outset than to tell someone he is failing.

Fitting into the church structure is essential to joining a church. People who find secure and significant places in the structure won't easily slip away.

For Review, Study, and Action

(1) Discuss the importance of security and significance in the church. How does your church provide for these two needs of new people?

(2) Which church-size description best fits your fellowship? What additional insights about new member incorporation could you add?

(3) Read 1 Corinthians 12:12-27. Make a list of insights which may help your church prevent dropouts.

(4) Discuss the various principles for small-group development in the church. Which seems most important to you? Which, if any, of the insights are new to you? How might these principles be used to help your church grow?

(5) Are there subgroups in your church fellowship? If so, list them.

(6) Are there groups in your church especially

designed to help new members develop a sense of belonging? How do they function?

(7) What is your church doing to help persons find their spiritual gifts? What is the "unemployment rate" in your church?

(8) How might your church find ways to provide meaningful involvement for all the members?

For Further Help

Spiritual Gifts Can Help Your Church Grow, by Peter Wagner (Regal Books). This book looks at 28 spiritual gifts, and how the exercise of each one can help the church grow.

The Care and Feeding of Volunteers, by Douglas W. Johnson (Nashville: Abingdon Press, 1989). This book gives helpful ideas for recruiting, training, and supporting church workers.

"Turning Committees into Community," by Roberta Hestenes *(Leadership*, Summer 1989). This article shows how one can deepen the human and spiritual dimensions of committee work.

CHAPTER ELEVEN

People Patterns

"One, two, three, four . . . fifty-five, fifty-six, fifty-seven . . . eighty-one, eighty-two, eighty-three. . . ." The shepherd had nearly finished counting his sheep. He counted the last stragglers. "Ninety-seven, ninety-eight, ninety-nine." Ninety-nine? There should have been one hundred. A sheep was missing! The shepherd looked around. He hoped to spot the missing sheep or lamb just outside the fold. But the missing one was nowhere.

Taking up lantern and staff, the shepherd retraced the day's steps. "Where might the sheep be?" The night was settling in, with its added dangers. Would he find his sheep safe and sound?

At last the shepherd returned home, bringing his sheep with him. He released it into the fold and breathed a sigh of relief as it mingled with the others. As the shepherd cared for his sheep, the Lord cares for his people. He goes to great lengths to bring strays back into the group (see Luke 15:1-7).

The Importance of Counting

Do you ever go fishing? If so, do you count your fish? Peter, Jesus' disciple, counted the fish he caught, at least sometimes. John 21:1-14 tells the story of Peter and his friends going fishing. They fished all night. Nothing.

Then Jesus came. He told them to fish on the right side of the boat. They quickly caught a boatload of fish —153 of them. Why did Peter and the others count? It must have been because they thought fish were important. Plus it impressed the people who read the story! Jesus had performed a notable miracle.

Earlier, in a scene by the lake, Jesus had said to Peter, referring to his ministry as an evangelist, "From now on, you will catch men"(Luke 5:10). On the first recorded occasion that Peter preached, 3000 people were drawn into the net (Acts 2:41). And Luke cited numbers to indicate that more and more people were joining the church (Acts 4:4; 5:14; 6:7).

People are important to evangelists—fishers of women and men. Sheep are important to a shepherd. The shepherd in Jesus' parable counted his sheep. That's how he knew one was missing. People are important to Jesus—important enough to be counted. Jesus wants lost sheep found.

How Do You Count?

There are a number of important ways to count people in a congregation. A good method is to count people present on a Sunday morning. Lyle Schaller, a church-growth consultant, indicates that worship attendance is one of the better indicators of congregational participation.[1]

Schaller offers nine reasons, several of which I will adapt and explain here.

(1) It's a sensitive barometer of the emotional and spiritual state of the congregation. Membership may

remain constant even as worship attendance fluc-
tuates greatly.

(2) It can provide a helpful comparison on a monthly
or yearly basis. In other words, it can show what
direction a congregation is moving in attendance.

(3) Worship attendance helps show how well new attenders are being incorporated as members. By
comparing total regular attendance with total membership figures, a congregation can judge how well
they are developing commitment in the church.

(4) Worship attendance provides a helpful index to
other numbers in the church. For example, you can
compare two sets of numbers, such as the number
of children compared with the total attendance.
Such comparisons can help congregations shape
programs or employ staff to meet growing needs.

It's also helpful to count first-time visitors every
Sunday morning. This indicates how well the congregation is doing at inviting guests. Or you might count the
number of visitors who returned for the second time.
This will give some indication of the first impression
you're giving visitors. People will come to visit on a
friend's recommendation. But only those who liked the
service will come back on their own.

Why Count?

Numbers are important only because each number repre-
sents a person made in the image of God. The Scripture
says: "Obey your leaders and submit to their authority.
They keep watch over you as men who must give an
account" (Heb. 13:17). Counting is one form of accountability.

What would happen if your church treasurer took
the same approach to financial accounting as to people

accounting? For example, the treasurer could say counting leads to pride. Or insist it would lead to a numbers game. Why do we count money? To sense our commitment to the Lord and the church. To see if we are making progress. To see if we are meeting our goals. To sense the enthusiasm of the members for the church.

All these reasons for counting money are also legitimate reasons to count people. God cares about people and numbers. *Counting is a form of stewardship, and people are far more important than money.*

Beyond Counting

There was a time when many people, particularly in rural communities, attended the same church all their lives. But times have changed. Even in many rural and suburban communities, there is much mobility. It's not unusual for people to attend many different churches over a period of years. Some persons refer to this phenomenon as the "circulation of the saints." One pastor commented, "Pastoring in this church is like ministering to a parade."

Such rapid turnover can cause congregations to overlook new members or short-term attenders. Who will miss them if there is no accounting for worship attenders by name? If they aren't missed, how will anyone show them pastoral care and concern? One solution, particularly in medium-to-large churches, is to have an attendance registry.

When introducing the attendance registry, Pastor Joe Sherer recalled his growing up on a dairy farm. His father kept a record of each cow. Joe reminded the church that a register of attendance is a way to keep track of people—who are more important than cows!

People can indicate their attendance on the fellowship registry each Sunday during the worship service.

Herb Miller suggests that attendance registration be done with the following instructions *each* Sunday morning:

> One of the things we value most in our church is friendliness. We want to know one another and extend a friendly welcome to those who worship with us. In order to help us do that, the ushers will come forward and distribute a "Ritual of Friendship" pad. We ask that you all, members and visitors alike, write your names and addresses. (Avoid telling them to *sign* the registration pad. That word *sign* has negative psychological connotations from military service and school memories.) When the pad reaches the inside aisle, please pass it back to the other end, noting the names and addresses of persons who are seated on your pew. This will give you the opportunity to greet and get acquainted with one another after the service.[2]

He insists that this announcement be made every Sunday so visitors understand the reason for writing their names. Even people who naturally resist instructions will write their names if the procedure is handled properly. The information on the pads can then be used to discern the people patterns in the church and to "watch over" the whole congregation.

Keeping Records

Particularly in a day when spontaneity in worship is valued, record-keeping seems dull and boring. But somehow, for the early Methodists, it imparted life. Keith Bailey writes, "Modern evangelicals often believe that regulations and records are the death of spirituality. History demonstrates that the absence of regulations and records are more likely to be the death of spirituality."[3]

John Wesley was rigid on promptness, requirements for membership, attendance, discipline, and record-keeping. He required new Christians to belong to a "class meeting." These class meetings were the key to real caring and accountability. Each class meeting had a leader who looked after each member of the group.

Keeping Computerized Church Records

Many churches have discovered that a computer can help keep accounts, both of finances and people.

Here's a sample of ways a computer could work for your church.[4] It can:

(1) Print a full set of church and Sunday school class rosters.
(2) Make lists of people who have missed three times in a row.
(3) Tell you whose birthdays or anniversaries are coming up.
(4) Tell you how many members there are and how many joined this year.
(5) Tell you who hasn't received a pastoral call in so many months.
(6) Print contributions statements as a year-end report for taxes.
(7) Tell you who is available to do neighborhood canvassing.
(8) Print checks for bills, then adjust the cash-on-hand figure.

However, a computer cannot:

(1) Smile and greet visitors warmly.

(2) Serve tea at committee meetings.
(3) Assign the most suitable committee members.
(4) Do follow-up calling.
(5) Work out disagreements between church members.
(6) Tell you who is growing spiritually, and who is not.

It's crucial that the computer program be compatible with your church's needs, interests, and goals. Otherwise, it will be of limited use, and may become a liability. If you want to try using a computer, consider these suggestions:

(1) Write out a purpose statement for your church.
(2) Write out a set of goals you are trying to achieve as a church.
(3) Make a list of tasks which you would like to be able to do with a computer, which can help to reach those goals.
(4) Find a person who can systematically and regularly enter data. (Without all the right updated data, your computer will be almost useless.)
(5) Shop around for church computer programs, and find one that will do the tasks you need.
(6) Shop around for a computer that will run the software program.

The Audit of Mission

Auditing is a way of dealing responsibly with financial records—to see that they are accurate and honest. Churches and businesses regularly have their financial books audited. But churches seldom audit their "people records" to see how accurately they reflect the life of the church.

A good auditor doesn't simply check facts. She will look at the system of record-keeping and see how well it's working. An audited report is often called an "opinion," since it represents an auditor's judgment of the financial records. Similarly, churches would do well to have an auditor judge their way of keeping "people records."

Some congregations have audited their entire approach to mission. For example, Mountville Mennonite Church in southeast Pennsylvania did this with the help of an outside agency. They did a comprehensive study to discern the changing "people patterns" in their church and neighborhood over a period of years. At a seminar, an outside consultant helped the pastor and congregation interpret the facts and decide what priorities to pursue.

Such a study can help congregations focus on their relationship to Christ and their community. In the words of another consulting agency:

> The undertaking of Mission Audit represents the recognition of mutual responsibility for the task of the church and a common accountability to the Head of the church for the obedient furtherance of the purpose of the church.[5]
>
> Insofar as disciples or congregations think they have nothing to learn or no improvements to make, they have already forfeited any claim to being disciples at all. Mission Audit is central to the discipleship of every person, group, congregation or institution bearing the name of Christian. Mission Audit is the process of listening to what we are, what we do, and how we relate with the world as it really is in the light of the overarching mission of God.[6]

Ask Newcomers How You Are Doing

As noted above, some congregations have benefited from systematically examining their church life and priorities to see how well they are incorporating new members. One way to examine your church is to discover how newcomers feel about it. And the way to find out is to ask.

Oswald and Leas studied assimilation patterns in a number of congregations. They determined that it's better not to have members interview newcomers to their own church for several reasons.[7] Perhaps the interviewee has had a negative experience with the interviewer or someone closely related. Or perhaps the interviewer will assume the answer to questions, based on previous experience. Furthermore, the interviewer may feel personally responsible for the newcomer's problems with the church. Feeling guilty or becoming defensive, the interviewer may block out information.

Oswald and Leas suggest that churches work together to interview each other's newcomers. Churches should be matched in terms of church size, denomination, cultural grouping, and philosophy of ministry. The two churches can then work together to decide what to study, what questions to ask, and how to report their findings.

By studying responses, you can determine ways to minister more effectively to new people. And you can work to change wrong patterns and become better stewards of the most important gift God can give a church—people!

For Review, Study, and Action

(1) Why do you suppose the Bible uses so many numbers? Can using numbers be spiritual? If so, in what ways? What are the dangers of counting?

(2) What kind of counting is your congregation doing? How are these numbers made public?

(3) How does counting relate to accountability? How accountable is your congregation?

(4) How do you feel about comparing counting people with counting money? How do they both relate to good stewardship in the church?

(5) What "people patterns" would be helpful for your congregation to see? How might you discern those patterns?

(6) How do you feel about Wesley's emphasis on record-keeping? What kinds of records does your congregation keep? How do you use them?

(7) Would a computer be useful in your church? Why or why not?

(8) How might a "mission audit" be helpful to your church?

(9) What congregation might you work with in interviewing new members? What might you learn from such a venture?

For Further Help

How to Diagnose and Renew Your Church, a seminar offered by Church Growth Incorporated, 709 East Colorado Boulevard, Pasadena, Calif. 91101. Churches who register for this seminar are sent a manual to use in gathering facts about the church and community. At the seminar, the facts are interpreted to help the church determine priorities for action.

Looking in the Mirror: Self-Appraisal in the Local Church, by Lyle Schaller (Nashville: Abingdon Press, 1984). This is a self-appraisal program for churches large or small.

CHAPTER TWELVE

Tradition, Tradition

Some people call me a "new" Mennonite—although I've been a member of a Mennonite church for almost a decade. Some say I'm a "non-ethnic" Mennonite, as if I have no ethnic identity at all. Still others insist my name just can't be Mennonite, as if the right family name is all it really takes to be one of the "in" group.

Sometimes such remarks annoy me. I want to go home and make faces in the mirror. Sometimes I think I'll change my name to Yoder. But at other times, when sanity and good humor reign, I just shrug off the comments with a smile. I like to think of myself as a *more-or-less* Mennonite.

I'm *more* Mennonite, for I made an adult commitment to follow Christ and identify with the Mennonite church. I share Mennonite concerns for peace, simple living, discipleship, community.

I also feel *less* Mennonite. I'm a third-generation Canadian with a Chinese background. I'm married to a third-generation Canadian with a Japanese background. I grew up in the city. When I bake bread it isn't *zwieback* but 100 percent stone-ground whole wheat. I don't understand hymns in German. I wonder why other people with the "right" names are claimed as Mennonites when they have little or no personal connection with the Mennonite church.

> So I'm a more-or-less Mennonite, not always sure where I fit in, not always sure I want to identify with everyone and everything that takes the name *Mennonite*. But the more I talk with people, the more I find others who feel the same way. There are many of us more-or-less Mennonites. We're Christians from a variety of cultural backgrounds who identify with the Mennonite church.[1]

These are the words of April Yamasaki, reflecting on her experience of trying to fit into the centuries-old tradition of the Mennonite Church. As she notes, it's not always easy to understand why things happen as they do in a church tradition.

It has been said that one can judge a church's receptivity to new people by observing the size of the church cemetery. This implies that a church becomes less receptive to new people as the church ages. It becomes more and more difficult for new people to relate to existing members of the church. And since traditions form and harden over time, it also becomes harder to make changes which would help the church thrive and grow.

Consequently, it's common for charismatic new leaders to form new churches and perhaps eventually a new denomination. But over time, what was once new and exciting simply becomes another tradition. In the Christian church, this has resulted in an increasing number of denominations.

Is there no other way to receive new members and implement new ideas? Are new churches the only ones that can receive new members?

No! While it's true that new churches tend to receive

new people more quickly than old churches, there is hope for old churches who want to grow.

Differences Between Newcomers and Long-term Members

There are significant differences between newcomers and long-term members. By recognizing these differences, churches can meet the unique needs of both new and old.

They have different reasons for being in the church. Newcomers generally come at the recommendation of a friend or in response to a special program. They may stay if they feel a personal need is being met.

Long-term members are there because they have formed a network of relationships in the church. They aren't likely to leave, even if the church program or worship services are less than exciting.

They have a different sense of ownership in the church. Newcomers feel like "outsiders." They find it hard to understand why members wrangle with each other about nitty-gritty details of church life.

Long-term members feel ownership of what happens in the church. Subgroups within the church may defend their own interests with a vengeance that puts off newcomers, particularly in congregational forums or council meetings.

They have different approaches to past events. Most newcomers have little interest in the church's history. Because they weren't a part of that history, they can't easily identify with it.

Long-term members, particularly those who have been deeply involved in the church, often have a deep interest in the past. They have likely invested both financially and spiritually in the life of the church. The stream of faces in the congregation's history come alive as they recall significant moments in church life.

They have different orientations to change. Because new members have little attachment to the past, they aren't likely to oppose change. If someone suggests an addition to the worship facility, they may well reason, "Why not? It will make room for more new people!"

Longtime members approach change more cautiously. They can recall the way it was done before. They may remember how things became the way they are now. Why change again? Moreover, long-term members know change may hurt. They may reason, "Why upset the harmony and balance that exists now by making unnecessary changes?"

They have different feelings toward the minister. Whether or not a newcomer stays after the first visit will often depend on the impression the minister makes. Unless the newcomer is attached to a small group within the church, the pastor and the worship service are the primary glue holding him or her to the church. The newcomer is likely to have strong positive feelings toward the pastor, particularly in a medium to large-sized church.

In contrast, the long-term member may or may not like the present minister. The present pastor may simply be the latest in a long string of pastors in the older member's experience in the church. Instead of leaving the church, a dissatisfied older member may try to help the pastor to leave! This may be particularly true if the pastor doesn't show appreciation for, and understanding of, the contributions made by long-term members.

They may have a different sense of enthusiasm in regard to church program. Newcomers are often excited about the church. If the church is meeting their needs, these "satisfied customers" may be the best advertisement for your church.

Many long-term members are also enthused. They are the people whose blood, sweat, and tears have built the church and sustained it. But some long-term members are less enthusiastic. Perhaps their hopes for the church have been dashed, their contributions have gone unnoticed, or their ideals haven't been met. They may dampen the spirits of new people coming in.

They may have differing attitudes towards the facility. Newer members are seldom drawn to the church because of the worship facility. Consequently, they're less attached to the worship facility or furnishings. They may even disrespect things that seem sacred to others.

Long-term members are more likely to be attached to the facility. It may be the place where they and/or their children were married and will be buried. The sights, sounds, and smells of the facility evoke good memories. Altering the facility and furniture may threaten older members who have "sweat equity" in the building.

People come to like a building for its very presence and the feelings it evokes. One pastor compared the church building to his wife's frying pan. It works better after a period of seasoning. This explains the disappointment people may feel in a new building. Although the architecture may be just right, it's not yet seasoned with memories.

For the newcomer, the church building isn't seasoned with those memories which may be powerful for the older member. It takes time for the newcomer to appreciate the artifacts so meaningful to the old-timer.

They may have differing attitudes toward denominational affiliation. Christians today are less loyal to denominations than they were earlier this century. The rising influence of nondenominational publishing houses, interdenominational Christian conferences, and contemporary Christian songbooks has eroded denominational differences.

Nevertheless, many new Christians remain in the denomination or fellowship of churches where they first found spiritual life. They may become strong denominational supporters.

However, long-term members born into a denomination will probably reserve the right to call themselves the true _____ (you supply the denominational name). They may not take kindly to an outsider or newcomer defining what it means to belong to their denomination.

Old and New Members Are Both Important

The church can be enriched by the contribution of both old and new. Growing churches recognize the ministry and meet the needs of both. What implications can we draw from the above study of the differences between older and newer members? I would suggest the following:

Both newer and older members have strengths and weaknesses. Newcomers may have visible weaknesses, particularly if they're new Christians. They may be sporadic in worship attendance. They may make promises they don't keep. Their lives may be an embarrassment to the name of the church. They may be insensitive to the feelings of people in the church. They may make seemingly irreverent comments about practices in the church.

Newcomers are also an important asset. New Christians represent the growing edge of the kingdom of God. Without new people, a church eventually dies. Their vibrant testimonies and newfound enthusiasm for following Christ can bring new life to the church.

Long-term members may also have weaknesses. An assertive pastor may resent some older members because of their seeming complacency and unwillingness to change. But treating older members as liabilities is a mistake. They may have good reasons for their opinions. Their counsel is important.

Long-term members bring stability. They follow through on promises. And while they may not be quick to affirm a new direction the pastor believes right, they won't quickly accept a wrong direction either.

Churches on the growing edge will find ways to help newer and older members appreciate one another's strengths and accept one another's weaknesses.

New Christians should be encouraged to give testimonies of what Christ has done in their lives. Especially at baptismal services, older members should be urged to either repeat the baptismal vows with the person being baptized, or make some other form of recommitment to Christ. Baptism needn't be simply a spectacle for people to observe. It can be a time for recommitment.

Older members should be lauded for their unique contributions. Public appreciation should be offered people who give time, energy, and money to the church. In this way, newer members will come to value the contributions of older members. When proposing changes, the leadership team should recognize those who have contributed to the present program, as well as those who have helped foster change. Recognition for a job well done or long service rendered will help older members open up to new ideas.

Older and newer members can both serve effectively in the church. In growing churches, there are many roles and tasks for members. Some are best done by older members or by mature Christians. Some can be done by either. The important thing is to see that both have a ministry.

New members should serve on a pastoral review or evaluation committee, if the church has one. Their positive feelings can be a real encouragement to the pastor.

It is helpful to have a mix of newer and older people on the church board. Since newer and older members have different strengths and weaknesses, both should be represented on church boards or committees. Congregations which have reached a plateau often wait too long to invite newer members to serve and offer new enthusiasm. Well-qualified new people may discover it takes years to have any influence in the church. They may then leave for a church where their gifts can be used.

Older members bring stability, a sense of the past, and a feel for the congregation. If the board has too many new members, some older members may begin to feel that they are no longer being represented in church decision-making.

Who Adapts to Whom?

What happens when a new person can't easily fit into the cultural and traditional patterns in the church? Who should make the changes? Who determines the best pattern? I pondered these questions after receiving a letter from a friend of mine. She wrote:

> I have noticed the term *assimilate* used frequently in relation to helping new believers become a part of our community of faith. I would like to suggest that another term may be more appropriate.
>
> To me, assimilate has a fairly negative connotation, maybe because I think of the scientific sense of the

word, as when an organism assimilates something as food for its system! I noticed the dictionary also lists "to absorb into the cultural tradition of a population or group" as another definition.

Do we really want to "absorb" people into our cultural group? This implies a sort of arrogance that what we have is bigger and better than any culture they may have. It suggests their own culture will be lost in ours. We should be aiming to encourage persons to become part of God's family without losing their own cultural identity. The lordship of Christ, not culture or tradition, should be our goal.

I think the word *integrate* more accurately describes the ideal process of a new believer becoming part of our church family. One of Webster's definitions of integrate is as follows: "to end the segregation of and bring into common and equal membership in society or an organization." Isn't that ideally what we are attempting to do, to "bring into common and equal membership"?

We can learn from new believers, just as they can learn from us. I see this idea of "common and equal membership" as crucial to our understanding of evangelism. If I were joining a group I would much prefer to be integrated than assimilated.

How about you? Which would you prefer?

When Tradition Is the Most Important Thing

Without tradition, most of us would find ourselves afloat on a sea of change, without a place to anchor our beliefs. But difficulties arise when traditions become too important in the life of the church. What are the dangers of tradition? More particularly, in what ways can an overemphasis on tradition or culture put up barriers against new people?

Ebenezer

It's common to find the word *Ebenezer* in church names. It has a biblical origin, deriving from an experience in the life of Samuel the prophet. After the Lord miraculously delivered the Israelites from their Philistine oppressors, he erected a stone marker to commemorate the spot, which he named Ebenezer, meaning (in Hebrew) "the stone of help" (1 Sam. 7:12). It was to remind the people that God had helped them come to that place. They couldn't claim to have done it on their own.

Every individual and church needs these Ebenezer markers to commemorate what God has done. It can be a great source of encouragement to see how far we've come, with the help of the Lord. But there is also danger here. It's possible to spend too much time looking back instead of ahead. The living God is still going ahead, leading the way to new places where more Ebenezers can be erected for God's glory.

Any church that spends too much time looking back will find it hard to keep the interest of new believers. They don't share the memories. By focusing too much on the past, we may lose sight of what God is doing now. Fixating on God's past action may prevent our openness to God's future action.

The problem of the third generation

When a church is new, membership may be carefully guarded. Those who join do so voluntarily. This is the situation depicted in the New Testament, particularly in Paul's letters.

By the third generation of a church's life, many members may have joined as children of the original members. If they hadn't joined, they would have been considered disloyal. Thus children of members generally find it easier to get into the church than do those from outside.

Stakes

Bobb Biehl tells of going to the circus as an adult. He looked forward to seeing the sights and feeling the thrills he experienced as a boy. This time, however, he saw something he hadn't noticed before. Full-grown elephants, capable of pulling huge logs through the forest, were tied to relatively small wooden stakes.

Bobb asked the keeper how it was possible to secure a huge beast to such a small stake. The keeper told him:

> It's easy when you know two things: elephants really do have great memories, but they really aren't very smart. When they are babies, we stake them down. They try to tug away from the stake maybe 10,000 times before they realize that they can't possibly get away. At that point, their "elephant memory" takes over and they remember for the rest of their lives that they can't get away from the stake.[2]

Those elephant stakes are like tradition. When a person comes to Christ and the church, she may be linked to a helpful tradition. But the memory of that tradition, and trying unsuccessfully to get away, may produce a bondage difficult to break. Perhaps the person should be freed from that stake for God's glory.

In the early days of the Protestant Reformation, a small band of Anabaptists were fleeing to a place of greater religious tolerance. They traveled with little means of financial support, having left many of their possessions behind. Their leader, Jacob Hutter, is said to have spread out a garment, inviting everyone to pool their meager resources.

From that time on, the group lived communally, taking as their biblical inspiration the example of the early church in Jerusalem. Communal living became a strong tradition and is now a defining characteristic of the Hutterites. One can't be a Hutterite without living in one of their colonies. They're tied to that tradition, which is like a stake. Young people who grow up in a Hutterite family must accept the tradition or leave the colony.

This isn't to argue against communal living, Hutterites, or tradition. It's simply to say that traditions can bind people. Let's be careful about tying new believers to traditions which may bind them for a lifetime, unless the tradition is essential and freely chosen.

Forging a great tradition

The Christian tradition is rich with the stories of God's acts in history. It grows richer each day as people around the world respond to God's saving grace and follow God in obedience. The greatest tradition a church can develop is to continually walk in God's ways, open to the new things God is doing. Part of that tradition is to gladly receive the new people that God entrusts to our churches.

For Review, Study, and Action
(1) In what way can you identify with April Yamasaki's feelings about trying to fit into a church tradition?
(2) Review the significant differences between older and newer members in a church. Which ones seem to be the most significant to your church?
(3) How have the strengths and weaknesses of newer and older members affected your church?
(4) What kind of word best describes the process by

which new people are brought into your fellowship? Assimilation, integration, incorporation, fitting in, joining, or absorbed?

(5) How can we tell when tradition is becoming too
important in the church?

(6) Think of several Ebenezers in the life of your
church. Does your church primarily look back to
those times, or forward to future Ebenezers?

(7) Discuss the problem of the third generation. Can it
be avoided? Has it been a problem in your church
fellowship?

(8) Ponder the idea of elephants and stakes. Are there
any stakes in your church life which should be
pulled out?

For Further Help

Liberating the Church: The Ecology of Church and Kingdom,
by Howard A. Snyder (Downers Grove: InterVarsity
Press, 1983). This helpful volume looks at the
church in light of Christ's kingdom. It's practical as
well as theologically stimulating.

CHAPTER THIRTEEN

Signing Up

The church was embroiled in controversy. The new pastor had made changes. Some people liked the changes, others didn't. Many new people had been drawn into the church, and more of them than long-term members were present. It was time to review the pastor's tenure.

The majority of the newer members (who had been drawn to the church through the pastor's ministry) wanted him to stay. Some long-term members preferred that he leave. The congregation took a vote of confidence. Many of the newer participants in the church weren't members and couldn't vote. The pastor lost the vote and resigned.

What are the implications of church membership in that story? How might the story have turned out differently if membership had been defined differently? What does membership mean?

The Meaning of Membership

The root of the idea of membership is found in Scripture. In 1 Corinthians 12:14-27, and in several other places, the apostle Paul likens the church to a human body. Each person is like one member (part) of the body. Every member of the body of Christ is a *member* of the church. One can't live dis-*member*ed any more than a hand or foot can live unattached to the body.

In chapter four, I noted that baptism marks entrance into church membership. In some places in the world, where Christians are despised, baptism and church membership indicate willingness to suffer for Christ.

But in many North American churches, membership is taken lightly. It implies voluntary association with a group. A member in good standing pays dues, obeys the rules, and carries out certain minimum obligations. Is there scriptural precedent for a membership roll comprising those willing to make meaningful commitments as prerequisite for membership? A further look at the apostle Paul's writing will help answer.

How the Idea of Membership Came to Be

Paul wrote:

> Are we beginning to commend ourselves again? Or do we need, like some people, letters of recommendation to you or from you? You yourselves are our letter, written on our hearts, known and read by everybody. You show that you are a letter from Christ, the result of our ministry, written not with ink but with the Spirit of the living God, not on tablets of stone but on tablets of human hearts (2 Cor. 3:1-3).

Apparently after Paul left Corinth to work elsewhere, the church began to doubt his credentials as a true apostle. In the above passage, Paul was apparently responding to a request from the Corinthians that he present a letter of recommendation from the "real apostles" at Jerusalem when he next visited. Paul asserted that he needed no such letter. His true credentials were amply demonstrated in the changed lives of the Corinthians themselves.

Although Paul needed no letter, he wrote them for others. A notable example was written to Philemon, pleading that he receive Onesimus into his household and the church fellowship. And Paul commended Phoebe to the church at Rome.

> I commend to you our sister Phoebe, a servant of the church in Cenchrea. I ask you to receive her in the Lord in a way worthy of the saints and to give her any help she may need from you, for she has been a great help to many people, including me." (Romans 16:1-2; for other examples, see 1 Cor. 16:3, 10-11; 2 Cor. 7:13-14; Phil. 2:29-30; Col. 4:7-13)

Letters of recommendation are apparently the fore-runners of today's membership letters—written when a person changes church fellowships. These are like the personal references employers usually require. A membership letter indicates good standing in a church fellowship and recommends that the person be received by the other church.

Most churches today don't request references from a former church. But such a letter could be helpful in two ways. First, a carefully written reference letter might help the new person find a place in the church more quickly. It could validate person's spiritual gifts and abilities. It could tell about the transferring member's ministry in the church. Second, a letter of reference could help the receiving church to be aware of special needs.

Contemporary Approaches to Membership

How have churches adopted the idea of membership today? What are the implications of the various approaches to membership? Consider the following three examples:

Dove Fellowship is a relatively new, growing fellowship. It has no membership roll. Any person who gives time, energy, and money is part of the church. A church directory is printed biannually, listing all the persons who regularly meet with one of the church's many house fellowships.

Group leaders are responsible for pastoral care. If persons drop out of attendance in a small group, and don't respond to the group leader's follow-up, their names are dropped from the directory. There are no membership meetings. The pastoral team makes the important ministry decisions, assisted by a group of elders.

At South Hills Community Church, membership in the church is almost synonymous with being a Christian and worshiping regularly with the church. A person fills out a membership card. Then he gives his Christian testimony to an elder appointed to give spiritual oversight. If the elder discerns that the applicant isn't a Christian, the elder presents the way of salvation. Many persons have confessed Jesus Christ as Lord and Savior in that setting.

In the early days at South Hills, there was no membership roll. But some newcomers felt a need for formal membership. Consequently, the church decided to simply "grandfather" the entire group of attenders into membership. Whoever signed a card became a member. Now, persons who want to join must go through a membership class. Some exceptions are made for persons already integrated into the fellowship who want to get on with some form of ministry.

In contrast to the first two examples, Communion Fellowship has a decidedly more structured and firm membership policy. To become a member, a person must accept six months' probation and sign a commitment form. In addition, each prospective member must attend a 12-week Christian basics class, then join a small nurture group.

Membership is reviewed and renewed annually. Any member who doesn't sign the annual membership renewal covenant is put on probation. This may last up to one year. At that time, a member either signs the membership covenant or is dropped from the roll. Only covenant members in good standing can vote.

Because of different emphases on membership, each of these churches has a different strategy for receiving new people into church membership. Regardless of a congregation's approach to membership, there should be clear guidelines to help new people become responsible members of the body of Christ.

Responsible Membership

What should you expect of people who join your church? What are the criteria by which to determine responsible church membership? You may want to consider ten characteristics of responsible membership to evaluate your own expectations of members in your church.[1] Responsible church members:

(1) **Grow spiritually.** Membership is not the sign of having attained some exalted spiritual state. It's a way to help Christians keep growing.

(2) **Are faithful in worship attendance.** Corporate worship is important for spiritual growth. Irregular worship attendance is a cause for spiritual concern. It generally indicates lack of commitment to the body.

(3) **Have many friendships in the congregation.** Body

life in the church should naturally lead to lasting friendships. People who develop deep friendships aren't easily lost to the church.

(4) **Belong to a fellowship group.** Unless the church is quite small, a large percentage of new members should find a meaningful place of belonging in a subgroup of the congregation.

(5) **Identify with the body.** Members should be able to say, "This is our church." When people use the pronouns *we* and *our* instead of *they* and *theirs* in referring to the church, they have identified with the body.

(6) **Have roles or tasks appropriate for their spiritual gifts.** Healthy churches have a high percentage of their people involved in roles and tasks.

(7) **Identify with the goals of the church.** Each local fellowship, under God, should determine a clear goal and direction for ministry. Identifying with the purposes of the church helps bring unity to the body.

(8) **Understand their values.** Members should be able to express their own needs and values in the context of the mission of the congregation. Members should be able to freely choose and prize the values for which the church stands.

(9) **Are concerned about stewardship.** Members who identify clearly with the goals of the church will give generously of themselves and their possessions to help reach the goals of the church, for the glory of God.

(10) **Bring other people to Christ and the church.** Members who are happy about their identification with Christ and the church will want to bring others into the fellowship. Members reluctant to bring others may be hesitant to identify too strongly with the church.

Perhaps these ten characteristics could be viewed as signposts pointing the way to responsible membership for new people who join. There is no better time to share your membership expectations than when new people are wanting to become members.

How Membership Commitment Contributes to Growth

What difference does it make what a church expects of members? Peter Wagner has helpfully explained some of the implications of membership commitment.[2] Using two terms originally coined in other contexts, he has shown how different membership policies reflect different values. These in turn affect the growth potential of the church.

Some churches function as a *modality*. People become members by living in the parish community, in much the same way children go to a school according to their district. And just as a mayor is concerned about the whole population of a city, so church leaders try to minister to the entire parish community. Simply being born into the parish grants members certain rights and privileges. *Membership requirements are deemphasized in favor of inclusiveness.*

It's easy for new people to join a church that functions as a modality. However, only a fraction of the membership may be truly involved in congregational life. One may be *in,* but what that means is unclear. On a given Sunday, there may be as many members absent as present. There is little sense of the gathered body of believers. The church may function as a "service station," where people come when they need something. Europe's state churches are classic examples.

Other churches function as a *sodality*. People join by meetings a set of requirements, similar to the way people join a club. Leaders try to minister to the needs of the voluntary membership. Only committed members have the privileges afforded by the church, such as voting. *A high value is placed on commitment and inclusiveness is deemphasized.*

To join a church that functions as a sodality, potential members must meet certain requirements. Even if they have been faithful members elsewhere, they may be required to attend membership classes. There is a strong sense of *in* and *out.* If people don't feel comfortable making the required commitments, they may feel excluded. But this kind of church often works hard to win outsiders and make them insiders.

Wagner asserts that churches and organizations functioning as sodalities have a much greater growth rate. This is because members are asked to make specific commitments to the church. For many years, Christian sodalities have taken the lead in evangelism. Some of these, such as Youth for Christ, Campus Crusade, and Youth With A Mission are well-known examples. Membership on staff implies a high commitment to the cause of evangelism. Persons who don't agree with stated organizational policy must leave.

Such a strict approach may seem counterproductive, but churches which function this way often attract highly committed people. Wagner cites the example of the Anabaptist movement of the sixteenth century, which grew rapidly as a result of functioning this way.

Membership Covenant

What kind of commitment should be required to join a church? How do members demonstrate that commitment to each other? The early English Baptists used a covenant which can still be helpful today: "We covenant with God and with each other, to walk in all his ways, known or to be made known to us, according to our best endeavors, whatsoever it shall cost us."

Patrick Baker, a Baptist pastor, will baptize only a person who makes a covenant with a local church. The applicant for baptism must become a member of a local church. So he has the applicant take vows entailing commitment to Christ and spelling out conditions for church membership. Some church leaders will baptize people without clarifying church membership. This can leave members of the body of Christ functioning in limbo.

Many denominations have written membership covenants. Many are long and complex. Because of high mobility, some have found it helpful to renew commitments to the covenant on an annual basis. The Church of the Saviour in Washington, D.C., is a notable example.

It's important that any church covenant not be too *idealistic* or too *legalistic*. The new covenant God makes with us is based not on laws, but relationship. Church membership should emphasize first of all a relationship with God through Jesus Christ, then a relationship with each other in the body of Christ. That's what it means to be a member!

Membership Classes

Because of the many different approaches to membership, there will be different kinds of orientation to the church. Regardless of the definition of membership, churches will do well to provide some formal orientation to the congregation. There are several elements to consider in the development of a meaningful orientation class:

(1) **An informal meeting of new persons** to help them get to know one another.
(2) **A series of scriptural lessons** which give a basic orientation to the beliefs and teaching of the church.
(3) **A list of opportunities for service in the church.** Take the opportunity to encourage a concern for the prosperity of the congregation.
(4) **A time of personal sharing.** Have new persons share their religious background, if any, and tell the reasons for their interest in your church. Allow them to share important memories. Ask for any expectations they may have of your church based on what they have experienced.
(5) **A personal profile on each new person,** identifying spiritual gifts, special interests, availability for service, and any unique needs.
(6) **An explanation of the history and policy of your church,** together with the present purpose and philosophy of ministry. Encourage new persons to ask questions about anything that may be puzzling.
(7) **An explanation of the membership procedures.** Help people find their way into the congregation. Prepare them for what it means to join your church.
(8) **A packet of materials** to acquaint the new person with the church. This may include the following: A pictorial church directory. A list of available small groups or activities. A brief history of the church. The church constitution and bylaws. A church facility layout plan with indications of uses for each room.

Whatever your plan for orienting new members, communicate the importance of a commitment to both

Christ and the church. By making membership meaningful, you can help members experience what it truly means to be part of the body of Christ.

For Review, Study, and Action

(1) Have you known a situation like the one described at the beginning of this chapter? How might a different approach to membership have changed the situation?

(2) Discuss the meaning of membership. What emphasis does your church put on membership?

(3) Discuss the biblical origins of membership. What kind of membership do you suppose the apostle Paul might recommend today?

(4) Discuss the various approaches to membership. If you were choosing a church, which kind of church would you be most likely to join?

(5) Discuss the idea of *modality* and *sodality*. Where does your congregation fit? What impact does your approach have on the way you welcome new people?

(6) Review the ten suggested characteristics of responsible members. Which are most important? Should other characteristics be included? How does this list compare with your church's expectations of new members?

(7) What do you think of covenant membership? Of annually renewable membership? Does your church or one you know use either approach to membership? If so, how is it working?

(8) How can the church best keep integrity in church membership? Does membership in your church, if you have membership, really mean what the church says it means?

(9) How does your church orient new people? How

many of the ideas suggested under the section *Membership Classes* does your church presently use?

For Further Help

A Third Way, by Paul M. Lederach (Scottdale: Herald Press, 1980). This is a stimulating theological study of the church in the Anabaptist tradition. It offers a strong emphasis on the church as an agency of the kingdom of God. Church members are called to be disciples.

The Call to Conversion, by Jim Wallis (San Francisco: Harper and Row, 1981). Wallis looks at the meaning of conversion in the life of a Christian. The author believes that the meaning of the gospel has been seriously eroded in recent times.

Bibliography

Arn, Win and Charles Arn, *The Master's Plan for Making Disciples* (Pasadena: Church Growth Press, 1982).

Bakke, Ray, *The Urban Christian: Effective Ministry in Today's Urban World* (Downers Grove: InterVarsity Press, 1987).

Dudley, Carl S., *Making the Small Church Effective* (Nashville: Abingdon Press, 1978).

Hale, J. Russell, *The Unchurched: Who They Are and Why They Stay Away* (New York: Harper and Row, 1980).

Harre, Alan F., *Close the Back Door: Ways to Create a Caring Fellowship* (St. Louis: Concordia Publishing House, 1984).

Hopler, Thom, *A World of Difference* (Downers Grove: InterVarsity Press, 1981).

Johnson, Douglas W., *The Care and Feeding of Volunteers* (Nashville: Abingdon Press, 1989).

Lederach, Paul M., *A Third Way* (Scottdale: Herald Press, 1980).

Mains, Karen Burton, *Key to a Loving Heart* (Elgin: David C. Cook, 1979).

Mains, Karen Burton, *Open Heart, Open Home* (Elgin: David C. Cook, 1976).

Miller, C. John, *Outgrowing the Ingrown Church* (Grand Rapids: Ministry Resources Library, Zondervan Publishing House, 1986).

Miller, Herb, *How to Build a Magnetic Church* (Nashville: Abingdon Press, 1987).

Mills, Brian, *Three Times Three Equals Twelve* (Eastbourne, U. K.: Kingsway Publications, 1986).

Moss, James W. Jr., *People Spots* (Eastern Pennsylvania Conference Churches of God, 1988).

Oswald, Roy M. and Speed B. Leas, *The Inviting Church: A Study of New Member Assimilation* (New York: Alban Institute, 1987).

Rand, Ron, *Won by One* (Ventura: Regal Books, 1988).

Schaller, Lyle E., *Looking in the Mirror: Self-Appraisal in the Local Church* (Nashville: Abingdon Press, 1984).

Schaller, Lyle E., *Assimilating New Members* (Nashville: Abingdon Press, 1978).

Shenk, David W. and Ervin R. Stutzman, *Creating Communities of the Kingdom* (Scottdale: Herald Press, 1988).

Snyder, Howard A., *Liberating the Church: The Ecology of Church and Kingdom* (Downers Grove: InterVarsity Press, 1983).

Stahl, Martha Denlinger, *By Birth or By Choice* (Scottdale: Herald Press, 1987).

Swindoll, Charles R., *Dropping Your Guard* (Waco: Word Books, 1987).

Swindoll, Charles R., *Improving Your Serve* (Waco: Word Books, 1981).

Wagner, C. Peter, *Your Spiritual Gifts Can Help Your Church Grow* (Ventura: Regal Books, 1979).

Wagner, C. Peter, *Leading Your Church to Growth* (Ventura: Regal Books, 1984).

Wallis, Jim, *The Call to Conversion* (San Francisco: Harper and Row, 1981).

Weeden, Larry K., ed., *The Magnetic Fellowship* (Waco: Word Books, 1988).

Wenger, A. Grace, and Dave and Neta Jackson, *Witness: Empowering the Church Through Worship, Community, and Mission* (Scottdale: Herald Press, 1989).

Zunkel, C. Wayne, *Church Growth Under Fire* (Scottdale: Herald Press, 1987).

Notes

Chapter 1

1. Here, and throughout the book, names are fictitious except when the context clearly indicates a real name is being used.
2. Jess Moody, *A Drink at Joel's Place* (Waco: Word Books, 1967), p. 18.
3. Ibid., p.22.
4. The questions have been adapted from those presented in a seminar, "How to Effectively Incorporate New Members," sponsored by the Institute for American Church Growth.

Chapter 2

1. These are adapted from "Win Arn Growth Report No. 20," available from 709 East Colorado Boulevard, Suite 150, Pasadena, Calif. 91101.

Chapter 3

1. This biblical explanation was given to me by Eddie Gibbs, a professor of church growth at Fuller Theological Seminary.
2. Jim Peterson, *Evangelism as a Lifestyle* (Colorado Springs: NavPress, 1980), pp. 76ff.

3. Win Arn and Charles Arn, *The Master's Plan for Making Disciples* (Pasadena: Church Growth Press, 1982).

Chapter 5

1. See Flavil Yeakley, *Why Churches Grow* (Christian Communications Inc., P.O. Box 238, Arvada, Colo. 80001).
2. Don and Judy McDonald, *Leadership*, Fall, 1986, pp. 72ff.

Chapter 6

1. James W. Moss, Sr., *People Spots* (Eastern Pa. Conference Churches of God, 1984, 1988) p. 90ff.

Chapter 7

1. Roy M. Oswald and Speed Leas, *The Inviting Church* (New York: The Alban Institute, 1987), p. 18.
2. Ray Bakke, *The Urban Christian* (Downers Grove: Inter-Varsity Press, 1987), p. 143.
3. Robert shared these ideas in a personal letter to me.

Chapter 8

1. Herb Miller, *How to Build a Magnetic Church* (Nashville: Abingdon Press, 1987), pp. 72-73.

Chapter 10

1. "Win Arn Growth Report No. 20," 709 East California Boulevard, Suite 150, Pasadena, Calif. 91101

Chapter 11

1. Lyle Schaller, *How Do You Count?* published in a booklet for the Institute for American Church Growth for a seminar on new member incorporation.
2. Herb Miller, *How to Build a Magnetic Church* (Nashville: Abingdon Press, 1987), p. 78.
3. Keith Bailey, *Care of Converts* (Harrisburg: Christian Publications, 1979).

4. Adapted from suggestions made by Rod Williams of Waterworks, 6115 10th Ave. S., Minneapolis, Minn., 55417.
5. *The Audit of Mission* (published by URCHIN, 115 Poplar High Street, London, E14 0AE, England), p. 5.
6. Ibid., p. 1.
7. Roy M. Oswald and Speed Leas, *The Inviting Church* (New York: Alban Institute, 1987), pp. 78ff.

Chapter 12

1. Taken, with slight alterations, from April Yamasaki, "A More-or-Less Mennonite," *Gospel Herald*, June 13, 1989, p. 406, and *The Mennonite*, June 13, 1989, p. 246. Used by permission.
2. Bobb Biehl tells "The Elephant Story" on the back cover of various materials from Masterplanning Group International, P.O. Box 6128, Laguna Hills, Calif. 92677-6128.

Chapter 13

1. The outline is adapted and developed from one suggested by the Institute for American Church Growth.
2. Peter Wagner, *Leading Your Church to Growth* (Ventura: Regal Books, 1984), pp. 141-161.

The Author

Ervin R. Stutzman, born as a twin, grew up in Kansas. He moved there from Iowa at age three after his father, Tobias, was killed in a car accident. Although he was raised in the Amish Mennonite Church, he affiliated in his later teen years with the Mennonite Church and is currently a member of Mount Joy Mennonite Church.

Ervin served for seven years as an associate director at Eastern Mennonite Board of Missions (Salunga, Pa.). His work related to church planting and evangelism. He presently serves as bishop in the Landisville District of Lancaster Mennonite Conference and as a resource person for the conference bishop board.

He is particularly interested in preaching, teaching, and writing. Recent publications include *Being God's People,* a study for new believers; and *Creating Communities of the Kingdom* (coauthored with David Shenk), a book on church planting.

The holder of B.A. and M.A. degrees, he recently finished course work for a Ph.D. at Temple University (Philadelphia, Pa.).

Ervin has a heart for church leaders and enjoys learning new ways of ministering to the needs of the body of Christ and sharing Christ's message. He also enjoys working with his wife, Bonnie, on woodworking and home-renovation projects. They have three children: Emma, Daniel, and Benjamin.